The Cloud and the Fire

His Path for Me

Doctor McLuskey with St Columba's Church of Scotland, London.

The Cloud and the Fire

His Path for Me

by

The Very Reverend Fraser McLuskey

M.C., M.A., B.D., D.D.

Formerly Minister of St. Columba's Church of Scotland,
Pont Street, London

The Pentland Press Limited
Edinburgh · Cambridge · Durham

by the same author:
Parachute Padre (SCM Press; Spa Books)

First published in 1993
Reprinted in 1994 by
The Pentland Press Ltd.
1 Hutton Close
South Church
Bishop Auckland
Durham

ISBN 1 85821 150 6

Grateful acknowledgement is made to the
Drummond Trust, 3 Pitt Terrace, Stirling, for
grant assistance in the publication of this book.

Typeset by Elite Typesetting Techniques, Southampton.
Printed by Professional Book Supplies Ltd. Abingdon Oxon. England

'And the Lord went before them by day in a pillar of cloud to lead them along the way and by night in a pillar of fire . . .'

(Exodus 13:21)

Contents

Foreword

by the Very Reverend Professor Thomas F. Torrance

This beautiful autobiography needs no foreword from me, but I am delighted to be associated with it for my admiration of Fraser McLuskey has continually deepened over the years ever since as fellow students in the University of Edinburgh we sat at the feet of Alfred Edward Taylor and Norman Kemp Smith in the Old College, and of Hugh Ross Mackintosh and John Baillie in the New College. Our paths were to diverge in the years that followed in war and peace, but they came increasingly together in the ministry of the Gospel, not least as the Church of Scotland called us to Moderatorial Office, and Fraser and Ruth came back to live in Edinburgh. When my wife and I read the typescript of this book we were both deeply moved, for we found it a spiritual experience to share with Fraser the joys and sorrows and spiritual pilgrimage of his life as a husband and parent, and as a chaplain and parish minister.

Although he writes very modestly about himself in this book the reader is given an unusual insight into the mind of one dedicated to the Holy. Ministry who from early years was increasingly conscious of a divine hand laid upon him, upholding and directing him through times of war and peace in the challenging services of Christ and his Gospel. This is very evident in the title Fraser McLuskey has chosen, 'The Cloud and the Fire', taken from the biblical account of God's redemptive deliverance of the people of Israel from Egypt, but also in the sub-title, 'His Path for Me', for together they indicate his profound sense of the fact that a Divine Presence has providentially led and protected him in the varying circumstances, dangers and exigencies of his life.

It is particularly striking that it is not upon himself that he really directs attention but to the Grace of the Lord Jesus Christ and to the Word of God which ministers of the Church are consecrated and ordained to serve. While ostensibly *The Cloud and the Fire* is an autobiography, it is actually a book about the theology of the Holy Ministry, as also about the changing patterns of ministry in the moral and social life of people today. This is indeed a very remarkable work of its kind for, while it does not shirk from difficult intellectual issues, it presents the theology of ministry in the form of an intimate and deeply spiritual account of the ministry exercised by one who has himself experienced the full range of what is involved, and in a way that can be readily appreciated by others whether they are ministers of the Gospel or not.

This is a work that will be widely appreciated by ordinary members of the Church for it gives them a unique insight into the essential nature of the Christian ministry. Moreover, it will, I believe, be especially valuable for those who are training to be ministers, for it offers a deeply spiritual and practical account of the ministry in which evangelical pastoral care is shown to be of rather greater significance than current emphases upon a ministry dictated largely by socio-political relevance. At the same time Dr McLuskey's frank and searching account of his own life and ministry will provide other ministers with a thought-provoking and refreshing means of reassessing and deepening their own service to Christ, not least in face of the spiritual hunger

that seems to lie behind the rise of religious cults and move-
ments in our contemporary society.

Preface

The story is told of a traveller who lost himself completely on a Highland moor. By great good fortune he met a gamekeeper out on his rounds. He was assured that he wasn't far from home and would soon be there. The guide set off with a confident step but he was having difficulty with his pipe. Eventually he admitted defeat and stopped to give it his undivided attention. At this point the visitor looked back over the ground they had covered together. To his surprise he could now see for the first time the outline of the track they had been following.

As I look back over the way I have travelled I am sure there has been one designed for me – often as I may have strayed from it.

> There's a divinity that shapes our ends
> Rough-hew them how we will.

For me, as for every Christian believer, that divinity is the God who reveals Himself uniquely in Jesus Christ. In a world filled with the wonders of God's Grace there is none greater than His will to lead us step by step and His ability to do so when daily we seek His forgiveness and strength. In the pages which follow I have tried to describe what I believe to have been His path for me.

That this book has appeared at all is due in no small measure to Marie Gordon, formerly my secretary in Bearsden. With the utmost patience and skill to match she typed the first draft. Wondering, as authors may sometimes do, whether publication should ever be sought I was immensely grateful to Helen Finch, distinguished writer and editor, for her encouraging appraisal. I acknowledge no less gladly my debt to my wife Ruth whose experienced journalist's eye has viewed the author's labours with invariable sympathy and understanding. Her company and affection, as those of my sons Kenneth and Andrew, have blessed the Path we have travelled together. It is an honour that *The Cloud and the Fire* should be introduced to the reader by the Very Reverend Professor Thomas F. Torrance. To him, now as always, my debt of gratitude is great.

Chapter 1

Schoolboy in Aberdeen

The railway bridge leading to Aberdeen's central station looked much as I remembered it some forty years ago. A chill autumn breeze swept up from the adjacent harbour. The solitary figure a little ahead of me seemed ill prepared to face it. As I drew level I could see he was an elderly man, poorly clad and worse shod. He looked as if he had been living rough and drinking hard. I walked on, feeling more and more uneasy, and then I turned back. I asked the stranger if I might present him with what seemed to us both a reasonably substantial gift. He accepted it gracefully. He couldn't know he had my father to thank for it. For one brief, agonising moment he was my father.

Not that my father drank. He was a life-long abstainer, whether from conviction or the fear of displeasing my mother I could never determine. It was hardly surprising that she was a fervent Temperance advocate. Her father had been a bad alcoholic and she could never forget the day he had lifted her up as a small child and threatened to drop her from an upper floor window. Good matrimonial relations apart, I doubt whether drinking had ever appealed to my father at all. Nor had he ever been a complete 'down and out'. Nevertheless, he ended his days shabby and poor, lonely and disappointed. In some very small degree I had been able to help and comfort him but it was

1

much too small. The gift to this total stranger was in large measure conscience money.

You could say it was mainly my father's fault that the McLuskey family left Aberdeen under what seemed to us a fairly considerable cloud. The small laundry business of which he was the very hard-working proprietor failed. This would have been bad enough anyway but there were additional complications. In a vain attempt to keep the business going he had offered shares to some of his employees. Now they were pressing for what they regarded as their legal entitlement and there was no money to pay them out. If proceedings were taken it might be judged that my father had acted improperly. The mere thought of such a possibility moved my mother, always highly strung, to a frenzy of anxiety, shared in some measure by my sister and me. In the event my mother's stepfather came to the rescue, as he had so often done in the past, and was frequently to do in the future. He cleared the debts and, so far as I know, there was never any court case.

If relations between my father and mother had been happier their marriage might have survived the crash. Over the years their troubles had grown. Money worries had a good deal to do with it. The business had been failing to yield an adequate income long before it finally folded up. This led to constantly recurring recriminations and scenes of which my sister and I were growingly conscious. Margaret was seven years my senior and had moved to her first job in Edinburgh three years before the final debacle, and so more and more my mother confided in me. Between the ages of fourteen and sixteen I was increasingly aware of problems on the home front. Tension mounted when something just had to be paid, like each term's instalment of the school fees. This amounted to what now seems a trifling amount but all the same there was frequently a frantic struggle to find it.

In many ways I could see my parents were devoted to each other and apparently free of other emotional entanglements, but they were so very different. Father was easy-going and not particularly ambitious. He had a very pleasant sense of humour which never deserted him even in the wilderness days towards the end of his life. He had never wanted to be a business man. His boyhood ambition had been to become a veterinary surgeon. A domineering mother had forced him into business, first apprenticing him to a jeweller and then introducing him to the laundry trade. Like my mother, he was a native of Edinburgh and there their paths had crossed. He was a presentable young man. I have a snapshot showing him beside the bicycle he rode proudly as captain of one of the cycling clubs popular at the turn of last century. He would escort my mother to her home after one of the concerts at which she had been accompanying her uncle, an accomplished singer. He was still singing, although no doubt with reduced volume, when I was old enough to do the same. 'Rocked in the Cradle of the Deep' was one of his favourites. 'Maire my Girl' was another. Mother often used to say she was attracted to my father because he was so respectful and never tried to kiss her goodnight, as no doubt other admirers had attempted to do – with what success I never learned.

The home which witnessed so circumspect and chaste a parting was a simple one. It had seen its own dramas through the years. My maternal grandfather was a cupar to trade and a man of some charm. He was said to be the best looking man to be seen on Leith Walk. He was an expert dancer and had an eye for the ladies. His drinking bouts brought out the worst in him and terrorised his wife and three daughters. His death was no doubt a release to them and in due course grandmother married again, this time George Scott, a countryman from Reston in Berwickshire. He set up business in Edinburgh, first in the fruit trade and subsequently as a potato merchant, achieving what appeared to the family a real degree of affluence. By this time my mother and one sister had married, while the youngest, an invalid for most of her life, enjoyed the devoted care which she and her mother ever received from Grandpa Scott. He proved a standby equally to my mother and to us all throughout his life.

When her school days ended mother had trained as a secretary, achieving and maintaining some fantastic speeds in shorthand and typing. Had she lived at a later period she would no doubt have taken a University degree and entered one of the professions. As it was, family circumstances, before the more secure Scott regime, made it essential that she start earning as soon as possible. There is no doubt that she was an extremely clever and gifted young woman and equally distinguished in appearance. She often told me how she had become the first lady secretary ever to be appointed to a firm of accountants, Martin Currie and Company. The partners at first were unwilling to contemplate a lady breaking into a wholly male reserve, but in due course mother won their complete confidence and indeed admiration. I learned this from the lips of one of the partners when, much later, I met him in Edinburgh. I suppose some of the difficulties in my parents' relationship arose from the fact that mother was much cleverer than my father, more ambitious, more of a personality. The tragic background of her early life made her subconsciously apprehensive of disaster and increasingly frustrated by her husband's inability to guarantee a secure financial foundation for the home.

The future seemed set fair enough in the early days of their marriage. My father had apparently been successful enough in his laundry training and became manager successively in Peebles, where my sister Margaret was born in 1907, then in Brechin, where things seemed to have gone well in every way, and then in Edinburgh, where I arrived in the fateful year of 1914. Thereafter he secured an appointment in Aberdeen, to which the family moved when I was an infant. I gather my father had grown increasingly restive working for someone else, and wanted to be his own boss. At all events, he later applied for and obtained the ownership of the small City Laundry which once stood on the narrow and crowded thoroughfare known as George Street. The business disappeared some years ago. From this point on, in spite of father's unceasing and heroic labours, the McLuskey fortunes proceeded to decline. Father was not cut out to be a business man, but even the most astute would have found conditions in Scotland in the twenties hard to overcome. The Coal Strike which preceded the General Strike of 1926 inflicted a blow on the small laundry business from which it never subsequently recovered. The only memories I retain of the Strike relate to the big boys in school who were old enough to drive buses and trams and engage in other 'blackleg' activities to their own enormous satisfaction.

The laundry itself played quite an important part in my young life. I was not mechanically minded but never ceased to be intrigued by the boiler house and what appeared to me the mighty engine which powered the different pieces of mechanism scattered over the three floors. They were always breaking down and I watched fascinated as Bob, a freelance and diminutive engineer, curled up inside one of the rotating washtubs to minister the necessary treatment. There was always a kindly welcome from the ladies, younger and older, who operated the presses and wielded the irons and emerged, apparently unscathed, from the steam-filled drying rooms. There was an overseer, Annie, who stayed with my father until the end and must have been worth her weight in gold to the business. My greatest treat of all was to be allowed to accompany the driver of the horse-drawn delivery van on his rounds and, on privileged occasions, to be allowed to hold the reins. At regular intervals there were lengthy excursions into what seemed to me the depths of the countryside. They may be reached in a matter of minutes now and no doubt oil boom Aberdeen has long since swallowed them up.

Comradeship with my father was by no means confined to laundry visits. I started my cycling life in his company on machines hired for each occasion. These were obtained at one of the strangest and most colourful emporiums in Scotland, or perhaps the world. It rejoiced in the name, among the locals, of 'Cocky Hunter's'. I am sure this reflected no lack of respect for Mr Hunter himself, who was certainly a gentleman of boundless enterprise. Slightly to adapt the Latin tag, it could be said that he considered nothing whatsoever alien to his interest and sympathies – always provided it was secondhand. Every conceivable article filled the floors of his establishment and overflowed in glorious confusion on to the pavement and street adjacent to the store – to remain there, I imagine, throughout the night watches, although I was never in a position to check this for myself. I am sure Mr Hunter was convinced that he could supply absolutely anything of any description whatsoever, if only he knew where to find it. We never made use of his omni-competent services except on those occasions when we needed to hire the cycles. A selection, perhaps a shade grubby and worn, suitable to every size and taste, invariably awaited our inspection outside the store. I think that an afternoon's outing cost a shilling for an adult and sixpence for a juvenile. How much I enjoyed these expeditions, and how vividly I remember that magic day when I acquired a bicycle of my very own! I think I was eleven or twelve and had waited for what seemed like an eternity until I was judged to be fit to cycle by myself. I can still share the thrill of coming downstairs at six a.m. to see the shining Raleigh of my dreams waiting for me in the hall. How indescribably exciting was that first ride on my own to the Esplanade before the city stirred! Even at the time I realised something of the inroads made by the purchase on the meagre McLuskey capital. Little as my father could afford it, he was determined that the bicycle should be the best available and it certainly was. It served me all through my school days with the seat heightened to keep pace with my growth. When in due course a Sturmey-Archer three-speed gear was added, my cup of cycling joy was full.

Whatever friction there may have been between my parents, they were at one in their determination to give my sister Margaret and myself the best education Aberdeen could provide. Margaret was sent to the High School for Girls and I to Aberdeen Grammar School. They were both staffed by efficient and dedicated teachers. Their principles were as high as their educational standards. It was assumed that the pupils were there to be taught and led by those well equipped to teach and lead. The results were and are encouraging. Both schools can be proud of what their pupils have contributed to this country as to many others. Both schools are now co-educational and have gone public in the sense that they are non-feepaying, and under control of the local authority. One would wish every boy and girl to be as fortunate in their schooling as my sister and I. One would wish every school to be as good as the High School and the Grammar most certainly were. Whether this will result from present social and educational policies, whether the levelling will be up or down, remains to be seen.

I was proud to be at the Grammar. I am sure that I was as well content to be there as I would have been anywhere else. On the other hand, I am certainly not in danger of claiming that my schooldays were the happiest of my life. At a very much later point, when my own University of Edinburgh was so kind as to present me with an honorary degree, the Dean of the Faculty of Divinity observed that as a student my main interests had been extra-curricular. That could well be said of my schooldays also. My real life was lived outside. As I entered my teens I acquired a lively interest, which I am glad to say continues still, in the opposite sex. The passage of some fifty years has not erased the memory of these charming young ladies. One in particular had a special power to haunt my Upper School years, raising me to the heights or plunging me to the depths at her will. Unfortunately from my point of view she was really more attached to another boy of about my own age. I am bound to concede that he was better looking than I, more athletic, more glamorous. The only thing I might claim to have been better at was ballroom dancing. I did have more than average aptitude in that direction and without doubt this was one of my main extracurricular interests. An evening at the Palais, when I was considered old enough to be there, with the girl of my dreams, was as near heaven as I ever expected to attain on earth. By present disco standards this may seem dull indeed, but was far from dull for me.

When I hear people going on about what young people today like to wear I recall how largely dress loomed in my youthful consciousness. My sartorial standards were set by two young men in the neighbourhood. They must have been in their early twenties when I was around fourteen. In appearance they were everything I longed to be. They wore tight-fitting, waisted coats. On very special occasions they appeared in black jackets, striped trousers, patent leather shoes and white spats. Sometimes the spats were spotted! The trousers were generously cut and left little space for the spats which peeped out coyly. Last but not least, they frequently sported yellow gloves. They both owned motor cycles and enjoyed a degree of affluence which was well beyond the reach of our little family. The lines of their mounts intrigued me. They had 'cradle' frames which meant that the rider sat low in relation to the handlebars. I found the arrangement aesthetically pleasing, like the waisted coats, the wide trousers and the white spats. I should add that sometimes my heroes appeared in plus fours, which, because they were very long and very baggy, appeared to me just right. For some reason shoes mattered a great deal to me. For what seemed a distressingly long period in my school life I had been condemned to wear boots. 'They strengthen your ankles,' my mother would say. 'That's right, sonny,' said my father. I can't recall his disagreeing with anything mother ever said, or ever calling me anything but 'sonny', no matter what my age might be. It was a great day indeed when I was allowed to graduate to shoes and even purchase a pair for myself at the sales. They were my own choice – brown, which was a great thrill, and in a style I can only describe as mildly streamlined. They were reduced to eight shillings and sixpence. I paid for them with my own money and never parted with hard-earned cash more eagerly.

No record of my lowbrow interests would be honest and complete without reference to the cinema. Often in the company of my parents and then increasingly on my own, I sat enthralled by the screen, for most of my boyhood days a silent one. We did have the pleasure of an orchestra, or at least a piano accompaniment, and then in more sophisticated times we watched the mighty Wurlitzer organ rise in all its glittering splendour, dispensing sweet music the while. Cinema seats then cost pence where now they cost pounds. This meant that I could just afford to be a regular attender, following closely the serials which were weekly features with their dramatic cliff-hanger endings and their understandably deflating and anticlimactic openings when the next instalment came along. What pleasure we had from Charlie Chaplin, Buster Keaton, Harold Lloyd. Laurel and Hardy were always my father's first favourites. I think the musicals were the ones I liked best, but for these, of course, I had to wait until the talkies started.

I suppose I might have been better employed. By present day standards the entertainment was wholesome enough. Violence, sex and the kitchen sink were still around the corner. In a sense there may not have been enough of the kitchen sink if that is taken to represent a concern for life as it is actually lived. I probably had too many doses of escapism, enjoyable as they were. My natural and still continuing tendency to transport myself to a fantasy world was reinforced rather than corrected.

I have no doubt that my teachers at the Aberdeen Grammar School did their best to that end. It must be confessed, however, that the longer I remained in school the worse I did. I had made a good start, gaining prizes all through the primary stages. I was equally successful on the rugby field until I reached my teens. Thereafter my academic and athletic performance dipped sharply. My ever loving mother provided the charitable explanation that I had grown too quickly, as indeed I had, and now was paying the price. Whatever the reason, I pursued a singularly undistinguished course through my five years in the secondary school. I followed the so-called classical stream, acquiring some knowledge of Latin and Greek along with French and the other usual subjects. I liked English and French as much as I disliked mathematics and science. I didn't dislike Latin and Greek but lacked the necessary application really to master them. I am sure I would have followed the classical stream anyway, being even less suited to any other, but it was considered particularly appropriate since even at this early stage I had accepted the idea that I should be a minister in the Church of Scotland. If the interest in my future profession occasionally seemed to me incongruous with the others I have mentioned at least it was no less real.

Nobody ever said to me that I ought to choose the ministry as a career, but conditioning factors are obvious enough. My mother, to whom I had always been deeply attached, was a very religious woman. Churchgoing and church activities had been an essential part of her life from her earliest days. It had always been her ambition and her fervent prayer that her only son might be a minister if that should be God's will. She was certainly the driving force in my life as in my sister's. Without any doubt she influenced me strongly in the direction of my subsequent vocation. My father was perfectly sympathetic to the idea. He was a church elder although not a particularly enthusiastic or active one. As elders go he was probably about average. In the Church of Scotland, as in Presbyterian churches generally, elders are men and, more recently, women, who are 'ordained', not to the ministry of preaching and the celebration of the sacraments, but to the management of the affairs of the congregation and the pastoral care of their fellow members. Home influence, ninety-nine point nine per cent my mother's, encouraged me to consider the minister's calling. Both parents wished their home to be a Christian one. We all went to church each Sunday morning. Normally my mother and sister and I went in the evening too. Sunday was not an unhappy day but clearly very different. Much that was apparently harmless and admissible on other days was ruled out. No Sunday papers, no playing the kind of syncopated music to which I was increasingly drawn. No cinema – even if one had been open. Sunday clothes and Sunday pursuits were taken for granted. Hymn singing was popular on Sunday evenings. Mother played the piano and father sometimes accompanied on the violin. When we were younger mother would read to us too: *Pilgrim's Progress* was a favourite, and *Line upon Line* too. Grace at meals was, of course, never forgotten. Like bedtime prayers they were part of the normal furniture of our lives.

In many ways it was a strict regime. My sister and I understood and accepted that we must obey our parents. In this case parents really meant mother since my father never seemed to make any demands. We knew that our school results should be as near perfect as we could make them. We knew that bad language should never cross our lips. We knew that Jesus Christ should be revered and taken as our example. Our parents could not have loved us more or done more, often at real personal sacrifice, to make life happy for us. We loved them deeply in return. Music and dancing lessons could ill be afforded but we had both from an early age. Our home was a hospitable one and always open to our friends. There were parties to give and to go to and musical evenings galore.

There was another factor of no less importance without which my life might well have followed a very different course. When I was ten or eleven the congregation to which we belonged in

Aberdeen, then known as East and Belmont, called a new minister, the Reverend James Kydd Thomson. He was an outstandingly gifted preacher, making the strongest appeal to young and old alike. Above all, it was abundantly clear that what he said meant everything to him. Here was a loving and lovable man with the most remarkable insight into the minds and hearts of his hearers. As I listened to his sermons and his prayers I found myself asking how it was that this man seemed to know exactly what my own personal problems were. 'Fraser,' he would have said to me, with his head tilted to one side as was his wont, 'I didn't know. Someone greater than you or I knew very well.' After 'J.K.' arrived I needed no urging to get me to church! I was glad to go. In fact I looked forward to it. It would never have occurred to me that I could ever be the kind of man my beloved minister had become but at least he had shown me what a minister might strive to be. He never asked me if I was 'saved'. He just showed me what it meant in his own life. He had not been in Aberdeen long when he became a family friend, dropping in quite often for a chat with my parents and my sister and me. We grieved with him when he lost his charming wife and could not fail to observe in what a deeply Christian way he bore so sore a loss. As things worked out, Mr Thomson was invited to a church in Edinburgh shortly before the family circumstances moved us there ourselves. This meant that all through my student days he could be with me still. No one, apart from my mother, did more to shape the pattern of my life.

Reflecting on these Aberdeen years, I realise we were in many ways most fortunate. We could have been called lower middle class. We moved home fairly frequently and usually under financial pressure but our home was always comfortable. We had plenty to eat and clothes which, even if less fancy than those on which I had come to set my heart, was entirely suitable to our station. Mother was a very hard worker and a very good manager who always knew how to make a little go a long way. I have dim recollections of days which must have been a good deal palmier when we had a substantial granite-built house, of which Aberdeen still boasts so many proud examples. At one time or another mother even employed a resident maid. By the time I had developed any real consciousness of the home situation we were clearly on the downward path. Maids were things of the past and houses progressively smaller. That we had one of our own at all was due latterly to the generosity of our long-suffering Grandpa Scott who provided the money for it. As my schooldays approached their end family outings for high tea and the pictures, or a visit to Harry Gordon's Beach Pavilion, grew less frequent. Tensions on the home front increased. My mother's anxieties and dread of the disgrace of bankruptcy produced a growing hostility between her and her husband. Father buried himself more and more in the tasks of the laundry and the unavailing struggle to pay staff and make ends meet. Domestic explosions became the order of the day. My mother confided in me more and more and, lacking any real understanding of my father's problems, I felt I must adopt a protective role towards her. By the time I was entering the fifth form and preparing for the Scottish Leaving Certificate Higher, the laundry business and my parents' relations were both on the point of collapse. I sat and passed the examinations in the spring of 1931 at the age of sixteen. Soon thereafter the business failed and had to be abandoned. Thanks to Grandpa Scott the debts were paid. With some sense of disgrace and virtually not a penny to our name we packed our bags and left for the comparative anonymity of Edinburgh where my sister, a tower of strength to us throughout, had contrived to find furnished lodgings in an area very different from those in which we had ever lived before. So ended, disastrously, the first sixteen and a half years of my life in Aberdeen. Little wonder that my return visit, to attend the annual reunion dinner of the Grammar School Former Pupils Club, set the bells of memory ringing.

Leaving Aberdeen in such circumstances was exceedingly painful for us all but I realise now that it was cruellest of all for my father. My sister shared our distress and could not have done more to help us make a new start. Nevertheless by this time she had made a place for herself in Edinburgh with a job she thoroughly enjoyed. My mother was apparently the most shattered by it all, losing the home she had worked so hard to create and a position in the congregation and the local community she greatly valued; but she still had her son and the ambition for his future which more and more dominated her life and his. Already she was planning to establish some sort of base in Edinburgh. The difficulties and disappointments were real enough but she was sure there was a future in which her dearest hope might be realised. As far as I was concerned, I felt completely miserable at the thought of leaving my friends and extra-curricular interests. I could part with school readily enough. I had long felt too grown-up for it. In a way I think I derived some comfort and satisfaction that our troubles had already bestowed on me a more grown-up role. In any case I was only sixteen and blessed with all the natural resilience of youth. My father was in the worst case. His business had failed and he knew himself to be beholden to his wife's family which had bailed him out not once but several times. Already in his fifties at a period of widespread unemployment, he could have little hope of a decent job. In fact he went from one unsatisfactory agency employment to another until he died, still in this partial harness. He accompanied us to Edinburgh and stayed with us except for those periods when employment took him elsewhere, but I suspect that he felt rather like an unwelcome and non-paying guest. His marriage had really ended. So far as he enjoyed any real relationship with the family it was with me. Only gradually did I grow to understand just how hard life for him must be. Only gradually did I acquire a rather more objective view of my mother to whom I owed and owe so much.

Chapter 2

Undergraduate in Edinburgh

I have no difficulty in recalling our main preoccupation as we settled in to life in Edinburgh. Our prime concern, over-riding all others, was simply to pay for a roof over our heads and to keep eating. An application for what was then called 'the dole' would have been considered the final indignity and in any case my father lacked the necessary qualifications. Already in his fifties, he had little chance of any satisfactory employment although he tried hard enough. Eventually his laundry experience led to work on a commission basis with firms in related fields. He was never able to do much more than earn enough for his own needs. My sister was by no means well off as a Youth Organiser with the Church of Scotland central offices. As the only earner in the family she was more than generous in the support she gave us all. Despite the change in our circumstances it was still the plan that when October came I should begin my course of training for the ministry. How then was any sort of home to be found and maintained? We knew we were fortunate to be lodged as we were but it was clearly a very temporary expedient. The only thing we could think of doing was somehow to obtain a house large enough to take paying guests. With any luck this would provide food and shelter for the six years' study which ministerial training then involved. Church of Scotland regulations then required that a first

15

University degree, normally in Arts, be taken before entering the Divinity Hall for the three years' theology course. We had no security to offer but once again Grandpa Scott stood in for us. After much searching a substantial three-storied house was found in the Newington area of Edinburgh, a pleasant residential district in the lee of Arthur's Seat. Number 2 Priestfield Road remained the family home until towards the end of her life my mother moved into a pleasant flat nearby. My father had already died.

The present availability and amounts of grants for university education would have seemed in 1931 as wild a fancy as spacecraft travel to the moon. Scottish students, however, were more fortunate than many others. Thanks to the benefaction of the Scottish industrialist, Andrew Carnegie, students could receive grants sufficient for the payment of part or all of their university fees as their needs dictated. I qualified for the full amount throughout my six years' course. Special provision had also been made in other ways to aid students proceeding to the ministry. An examination for scholarships could be taken prior to the Arts course and for this I spent my first few months in Edinburgh preparing. The thought of hanging is said to have the effect of wonderfully concentrating the mind. Economic pressures clearly had a similar result in my case. I was awarded what seemed to me a substantial amount payable each year until my studies ended. The sum actually increased when I became a divinity student and carried with it the obligation to tutor in New Testament Greek. In addition to scholarships obtained by examination there were, and no doubt still are, a number of bursaries available for presentation. I applied for and obtained several of them. I remember that one was called the Dall Bursary and I qualified for this for no other reason than that my parents had once lived in Brechin. There was a stipulation, by no means unreasonable, that the bursar should at some stage conduct divine service in the church in Brechin to which the generous donor had himself belonged. I well remember going to pay my dues in this way when my theological course was well advanced and hoped that I would be judged worth the money.

I knew my first responsibility was to prepare for the scholarship examination but I was keen to earn at least a little money as soon as possible. My grandfather's potato business provided an opportunity. By this time I suppose I had had time to catch up with my early rapid growth, the hundredweight bags presented no problem and I found the whole experience very agreeable. I had the delightful companionship of John Reynolds with whom I immediately established a firm friendship. He had been in my grandfather's employ for many years and in every sense was his right hand man. He drove the lorry, a T model Ford, and loaded and unloaded enormous quantities of potatoes with an ease and skill I never ceased to admire. He was enormously good natured and although I was still sixteen and so below the age required for a driving licence, he somehow found opportunity to teach me to handle the Ford which he well knew I was aching to do. We supplied a number of fruit shops in different parts of the city but our main customers were the proprietors, in most cases Italian, of fish and chip shops. I became well acquainted with the subterranean cellars in which we dumped our load and with the tortuous and treacherous stairways which led to the evil smelling depths. John was the hardest of workers but even he required a break for nourishment occasionally, much to my relief. In those days the larger size of individual mutton pies cost twopence. I think a cup of tea cost the same at least in the cafés we frequented. In days when a 'good' take-home wage might well be in the region of two pounds, a working man could hardly have been expected to pay more.

I discovered John was a man of parts. He usually carried a number of little booklets which were propped up in turn on the

Ford dashboard. These were the textbooks of the Christian Endeavour Movement, of which John was an enthusiastic devotee. The organisation had its own grades of membership and John was continually studying to take a step up. To do so it was necessary to know by heart the catechisms which the booklets contained. I had little expected to engage in discussions of Christian doctrine when I first took my place on the lorry beside its burly driver.

Grandpa Scott was not our only kind friend in these somewhat traumatic days of transition. We had introductions to two men who came to take the most helpful interest in the McLuskey fortunes. As youngsters will, I found some entertainment in the fact that one was called Nightingale and the other Lightbody. Charles Nightingale was a distinguished Edinburgh solicitor who took us under his legal wing and remained our valued counsellor until his death. He was a keen Methodist and was honoured by the Vice-Presidency of their Assembly. I remember him speaking with a mixture of caution and admiration of Donald Soper, as he then was. I gathered that this Mr Soper was just a trifle too way-out for this most polished and conservative representative of his profession. Mr Nightingale shared with my mother an enthusiastic support of the Temperance cause. When he arranged for me to take out my first life assurance he commended the special terms offered to total abstainers. Many years later I felt obliged to be transferred to the general section and it says much for this most gracious Christian man that the warmth of his friendship continued unabated.

It was thanks to Mr Nightingale that I met Mr Lightbody. He was then, and for many years to follow, the Secretary of the Scottish National Council of YMCAs. As corpulent as he was kindly, he had a swarthy, sea-lion type of countenance in which his beady eyes tended to disappear from view. I was referred to him in the hope that he might find me summer employment.

This he immediately proceeded to do and for each succeeding summer of my student days I toiled on the staffs of the YMCA serving the needs of Territorial encampments. In the camps with which I was concerned in Scotland we were always under canvas which meant much hard labour in the erection and dismantling of the enormous marquee in which we conducted our business. In Catterick in Yorkshire where for several summers I was employed by the English YMCA, we had the luxury of huts, relics of World War One. The idea was to provide light refreshments at stated hours during the day and during the evening and to make the marquee or hut as homely as possible. In addition there was usually an epilogue, a brief act of worship at the close of each evening, and an informal service on Sundays. The set-up will be familiar to Servicemen of any generation. The practical advantage from my point of view was that while I was engaged in this work I lived and ate at the YMCA's expense and was not, therefore, a mouth to feed at home. There was no pay but at the end of each summer's camp I received an honorarium. If it was as much as ten pounds I felt rich indeed. It was an education in itself to meet the varied types of men who had volunteered to give service in the territorial units for which we catered. We little thought that before very long the worth of their training would encounter such a test. Not least, I started to overcome in some small measure the nervousness which had always made any kind of public appearance a nightmare to me. It was to take a very long time indeed before that problem could be overcome.

By the time the University session opened our home was a going concern. My sister had introduced two of her colleagues who required accommodation and one of these brought her sister. Either then or shortly afterwards we were invited to receive three children whose parents were missionaries in Manchuria, as the country then was known. In what seemed to us a strikingly providential manner the supply of missionary families continued through the years. We would have been grateful to have had any guests at all to keep the business afloat. We were specially thankful to have so many young people who greatly needed the home we tried hard to provide.

Against such a background my six years as a student pursued their interesting and enjoyable course. Had our circumstances been different, and had the University been residential, the experience would no doubt have left a much deeper mark on me. No more a philistine than the next man, I nevertheless viewed the acquisition of the two degrees involved principally as a passport to economic independence. I might almost have said wealth. When we arrived penniless from Aberdeen in 1931 the minimum rate for the minister's job was three hundred pounds a year, plus a manse. This really looked like affluence when viewed from our perilous position. As a matter of fact it was at that time quite a reasonable remuneration. The present scales compare very ill when real money values are taken into account. I approached my undergraduate days with a business-like attitude. I had to get through, and I had to get through with the maximum speed possible. Learning for learning's sake cannot be said to have loomed very large. No one suggested that I might take a four year Honours course instead of the three year Ordinary degree, but if they had the idea would not have been entertained for a moment. It seemed little short of miraculous that I could have the opportunity of a university education at all. To have extended it beyond the minimum period would have seemed absurd. When, barely one month after my seventeenth birthday, I reported for Latin, Greek and English classes which were first on the list it was with an almost grim determination to get on and get out. In the unemployment situation in Scotland in the hungry thirties my attitude was certainly not unique.

The scholarly men and women who presided over our studies did their best to widen my horizon. They were much too gifted to fail. Professor Herbert Grierson was still teaching in my day. I can still hear his voice as he stood side on to the classroom, pulling on his ample jowel and reciting in vibrant, organ-like tones, '*Timor mortis conturbat me.*' No doubt what he had to say might have been read in one of his books but how much it meant to a youngster such as myself to see and hear such a man and to gain at least some insight into so rich a personality. When I took the Second English class the following year the numbers, though still large, were of more manageable proportions and something in the nature of a tutorial system could be operated. Neither Professor Calder of the Greek class nor Professor Richmond of the Latin held the magic of Grierson as far as I was concerned but both opened my eyes at least to some degree to a culture, a philosophy, a way of life, a way of thinking, as well as to a language.

We are all tempted, as we look back, to assert that there were giants in those days. I must claim a certain justification. Norman Kemp Smith taught Logic and Metaphysics, to give the Philosophy class its proper name. The subject fascinated me as well it might in the hands of one of its greatest exponents. Even more I enjoyed the Moral Philosophy class which I took in my third year. A.E. Taylor, already enjoying worldwide renown, shuffled into the classroom, a small, dishevelled, quaint figure of a man, and proceeded to hold us spellbound. It was the only subject in which my essays received any grade of distinction. I found myself wishing that I didn't have to rush through the course, that I could have stayed on in this department of studies for another year or two. But I never supposed this was more than an idle dream. Life was stern and life was earnest. More important still, life was costly and we needed the cash and needed it quickly.

It would be entirely misleading if I were to suggest that my undergraduate days were always stern and always earnest. This was very far from the case. During these three years I had a very good time and enjoyed it immensely. I never became a first class rugby player, but I did improve to the extent that on a number of occasions I was chosen to represent the University and sufficiently often to be awarded eventually a half-blue, known in Edinburgh as a Green. Rugby was one of my main interests. How vividly I recall scanning the appropriate notice-boards each week to see in which team, the first or the second, I had been chosen to appear. I devoted a good deal of time also to training sessions in the University gymnasium. I appeared on the scene just as organised classes were starting under the keen eye of Colonel Ronald Campbell who was to become to me as to so many other students an invariably kind and fatherly friend. My addiction to the gym must have been noticed by my student friends. At least on one occasion I achieved a short-lived fame by appearing in limerick form in the student magazine concerned with athletics. To rhyme with the awkward name of McLuskey it was stated that at rugby I was decidedly husky. The poet then went on to add that I was a positive vulture for physical culture. I am thankful to say that the keep-fit complex has not as yet deserted me.

Then as now there was a rich variety of University societies. The only one with which I made any lasting connection was the Student Christian Movement. The organisation has experienced a good many vicissitudes through the years and it is at least open to doubt that it has survived very satisfactorily. In the thirties there could be no doubt whatsoever that it was a tremendous force for good in the universities of this country as in others. Its expressed aim was to help students to understand the Christian faith and to live the Christian life. For me as for so many others it fulfilled that aim admirably. Where the parallel organisation, the Inter-Varsity Fellowship of Evangelical Unions, tended to a fundamentalist position and attracted on the whole Christians of a rather narrower background, the Student Christian Movement opened its doors wide enough to welcome any seeker after truth. It worked very largely through study groups in which the members could read and discuss together. It was staffed by keen and dedicated young secretaries little older than the students they sought to shepherd. It was inter-denominational. In place of the Keswick type of convention the annual Swanick conference provided opportunity for search and discussion in a more concentrated fashion. Leading Christian thinkers read papers and directed our acts of worship. It is common knowledge that the SCM of this period provided most of the pioneers in the ecumenical movement in this country as in others. Tissington Tatlow, the first and legendary General Secretary, had already retired when I joined the movement but he was still around and I sometimes heard him taking part in the General Council of which I was a student member. Indeed, apart from the secretaries, we were all students. This fact largely accounts for the vigour and spontaneity and growth which characterised the movement in these days. The General Secretary was then the Reverend Robert C. Mackie, a minister of the Church of Scotland and one of the truly great Christian leaders of our day. He later moved to be a Secretary of the World Council of Churches in Geneva and so served alongside Dr Visser T'Hooft who had earlier been General Secretary of the World Student Christian Federation, the international SCM body. Oliver Tomkins, eventually to be Bishop of Bristol, was Study Secretary. Bishops, Deans, Moderators, Christian missionaries in every quarter of the globe, all bear witness to the influence of the SCM in the thirties and earlier. I shall never cease to be thankful that Hamish Alexander, later a missionary in Africa and thereafter secretary of the Scottish Bible Society, called on me when he was a senior student and I had scarcely enrolled and invited me to the SCM Freshers' Social. I owe much more than I can assess to meeting regularly with students of different faculties and different denominations for Bible Study and for discussion of social and international concerns. Prayer was an integral part of our fellowship, prayer led by young people like myself in language I could understand and concerned with problems meaningful to us all. It meant that I could never thereafter think of the Christian Church in terms of one denomination only or doubt that branches other than my own had rich gifts to offer. One of the travelling secretaries whose visits meant much to us was Lesslie Newbigin, subsequently an architect of Church union in South India and one of the most original and creative Christian thinkers of our day.

The University had its own flourishing social life centring in the Men's and Women's Unions. I don't think there was any strong feeling that the Unions should be mixed. I never joined the Men's, partly because my home was only walking distance away, and even more because pounds and shillings had to be counted carefully. Coffee in Martin's, a baker's and tea-shop on the Bridges almost opposite the Old Quad, was usually within my means and apparently they even stretched to the entertainment of the student girl friends whose company so considerably brightened my academic pursuits. One I remember with continuing affection lived in a residence for women students and invited me to the hostel dances. Edinburgh, I am glad to say, had its Palais too, in Fountainbridge, and there was time and money enough for at least an occasional visit with the partner of the moment. No very serious attachment was to develop at this stage. My young and extremely vulnerable heart was still with my charmer in Aberdeen.

Meanwhile our guest-house was prospering. At least that's how it seemed to us. We were clearing our costs and providing for all necessary living expenses. Towards the end of my undergraduate days I even managed to acquire and run an Austin Seven, fabric body. I bought it for what seemed to me the fair and substantial sum of £7 10s. It was only seven or eight years old and I considered it in splendid condition. The cheapest petrol at about a shilling a gallon kept it chugging along for at least forty miles. With the annual licence costing, I think, five guineas and insurance rates small even by my impecunious standards, I could just manage to afford it. There was still the odd job on the potato lorry and for a period the opportunity to do some tutoring in Latin with a pupil even less erudite than I was. One way or another through my student days I managed to own some sort of a vehicle. A succession accompanied me through my days at New College. One in particular I can never possibly forget. It was a very large and ancient Wolseley saloon. It went like a bomb but in the process swallowed so much oil that I could only make any journey, however brief, by carrying a large oil drum in the boot. I think I enjoyed its company for weeks rather than months.

One at least of my boyhood dreams had been fulfilled. I had a car of my own to drive. Another was to have a dog once again. The smooth-haired fox-terrier who enlivened our days in Aberdeen had died before we left. My father and I had shared his care and were both equally unsuccessful in instilling the slightest rudiments of good behaviour into his highly intelligent head. Chasing passing cyclists and attacking dogs larger than himself and even larger postmen were his principal joys. The Airedale who joined our family circle in Edinburgh was a very different character. By that time I had more of an idea what dog training was about. Corrie reacted well to my efforts and proved an excellent companion as we roamed the length and breadth of the King's Park and Blackford Hill, both within easy reach. We all have our faults and two of these Corrie proved quite incapable of leaving behind her. She could never resist exploring any dustbin within sight or scent. Even worse, she simply had to roll herself in whatever dirt the streets and pavements might yield and the more evil smelling the mixture the better she seemed pleased. It says much for our mutual affection that it survived even the strain introduced by such extremely unlovable addictions.

Chapter 3

Student for the Ministry

Candidates for the ministry of the Church of Scotland today must pass a selection board. No such system was in operation when I applied for admission to New College in 1934. If one held a University degree, as I then did, and was adopted as a candidate by the local court of the Church of Scotland known as the Presbytery, then all was well. On arrival we did have to write an essay describing our call to the ministry. Thereafter we were interviewed by the College Principal, the Very Reverend Dr Alexander Martin, who commented on what we had written. I think he found my statement somewhat unsatisfactory. I have no idea just what I said, but not unnaturally I had mentioned the influence of a Christian home and the inspiration of my own minister through the years. I think I said, too, that I had assumed I would be a minister from quite an early age. He indicated that all this was not enough. Could I not point to any decisive spiritual experience which might constitute an undeniable call? I don't think I could, but nevertheless Principal Martin charitably refrained from ordering me to the door. Perhaps he thought that the College course over which he presided could be relied upon to fill in any unfortunate spiritual gaps.

I found the interview somewhat disconcerting. Here was someone in authority who was not overwhelmed by the conviction that James Fraser McLuskey was clearly God's special gift to the Church. How right this wise and scholarly Christian man was to challenge me to ask this fundamental question as to my vocation. Without the sure conviction that, despite my unworthiness, God wanted to use me in this way, what right had I to be entering on this course at all? I think in my own way I did have that conviction although I found it hard to put it into words. Nor had there been any one occasion when I had heard God say plainly that this was His plan for my life. The conviction had grown gradually as life had gone on. I had no doubt I was meant to be a minister although there was no dramatic turning point on which I could put a finger. I remembered this often in years to come when the subject of conversion was under discussion. It is not given to everyone to experience the kind of confrontation with Jesus which came to Paul on the road to Damascus. We are all different and so it is hardly surprising that God speaks to us and calls us to His service in very different ways. It is a mistake and a most unfortunate one to assume that there must be one standard pattern to which we must all conform if we claim to be Christians. A meeting with Jesus there must certainly be and a conscious decision to take Him as Master. Thanks to a Christian home that first meeting came very early for me and I cannot remember a time when I did not know that Jesus had to come first, although often He failed to do so.

New College is housed in the Assembly Buildings of the Church of Scotland in Edinburgh which occupy a commanding position on the Mound adjacent to the Castle. This means that Divinity students have a life of their own at some small remove from the undergraduate throng in the Old Quad. The College was non-residential which had both advantages and disadvantages. We were in no·danger of monastic seclusion. We were still very much part of the University and city. On the other hand we might have profited from the disciplined routine a residential college makes possible. If a minister is to help others with their life of prayer he needs any help he can get towards the organisation of his own. Daily College prayers as I remember them were not a great aid to this end. We did have some degree of communal life. Classes were all held during the morning and thereafter most of the students and some of the staff met for lunch. A Common Room was available for use during breaks between classes and housed the student societies which normally met during the afternoon. At least to a limited extent we felt ourselves to be a band of brothers. Numbers were small. There were thirty in my year. Undergraduate days were behind us. We were all there for the same purpose, to train for the work of the ministry at home or overseas. Those who did decide on overseas service received additional training at St. Colm's Missionary College.

There were four departments of study concerned with the Old Testament, the New Testament, Church History and Theology. All students were expected to reach the necessary level of competence in each branch. As Old Testament studies involved some knowledge of Hebrew and the New Testament required Greek a certain amount of hard work just had to be done. Hebrew is no longer obligatory for every student but I cannot believe any lasting damage to the progress of the Christian cause is likely to result. It is arguable, too, that for most students who are non-specialists the time spent on Greek would be more usefully spent in learning how to make the best possible use of the rich variety of modern versions of the Bible and the many excellent commentaries now at our disposal. Those who teach either subject need not feel insecure. It will always be necessary for those who wish to become Old or New Testament scholars to acquire a thorough knowledge of the languages in which the books of the Bible were originally composed. In the thirties, and I think still today, students who aimed to take the degree of Bachelor of Divinity were required to specialise in one department of study. It was not necessary to take the degree. The satisfactory performance of the prescribed work each session meant that licensing would follow by the Presbytery under whose care the individual student was placed. At the conclusion of the College course students who had satisfied the examiners and had been 'licensed' were termed Probationers. They were 'licensed' to preach but not to administer the two Sacraments recognised in the Church of Scotland, Baptism and Holy Communion. Permission to exercise that further ministerial function had to await their Ordination which normally took place when they were inducted to their first parish.

I had worked as hard as I could as an undergraduate so as to be quite certain of getting my degree in the shortest possible time. Now it was a very different situation. Some of the pressures were removed. I was within sight of my goal. Having reached the ripe age of twenty I felt inclined to examine my teachers with a slightly more critical eye. Of course, every member of the staff was an extremely competent scholar but that is not necessarily the same as being a good teacher. There was a temptation, which I fear I did not always resist, to switch off when the lecturer was dull. I realised later that this was very much to my own loss and under the pressures of the work in which I had by then become engaged acquired a new respect for some of my mentors to whom I had given less than my closest attention. At least this should prove, in the unlikely event that proof should be required, that divinity students do not automatically become paragons of perfection by the mere process of enrolment in a theological college. Some trace of their unredeemed undergraduate days clings to them still. It certainly did to me.

Two men never failed to rivet my attention. Between them they laid the foundations of such theological understanding as I may now possess. H.R. Mackintosh taught Dogmatics, the study of the content of Christian doctrine. It was said that entering his classroom felt just like going into church. There was an atmosphere of reverence one sensed immediately. Here was a man of the most profound scholarship whose theological teaching was wholly Christ-centred for the very good reason that he was himself Christ's man in heart as in mind. The Christian doctrine he expounded to us with such clarity and felicity of expression was his own living faith. This man of letters was a man of God and not one of us failed to understand the fact. We admired him for his erudition. We revered him for what he was in himself.

Serious as was his normal mien, H.R. was by no means devoid of humour. Some light relief was occasionally obtained during the sermon class which he conducted. Each week one student was chosen to deliver, not a whole sermon (that might have been too much for the student and the class and possibly also for our Professor), but a sermon synopsis lasting seven minutes. Two other students were appointed critics and were required to give their reactions. Expecting to be in the position of preacher themselves in due course, their comments were no doubt informed by caution as well as charity. Thereafter H.R. himself pronounced on the whole exercise. Occasionally the master's verdict could be devastating. I don't think any of our class will ever forget the day when one of our number, having delivered his synopsis, was asked by the Professor in his usual measured tones which commentaries he had consulted in the preparation of his discourse. The student answered that as it happened he had consulted none. A deathly silence ensued. 'That, gentlemen,' said H.R., speaking slowly and with great deliberation, 'is the unforgivable sin.' I doubt whether any who shared this thunderbolt were able ever afterwards to address their congregations on any passage of Scripture without making at least some prior attempt to ensure that they themselves knew what the passage really meant.

John Baillie was a much younger man and had himself been a
student of Mackintosh in earlier days. He came to New College, just as I arrived there, from Union Seminary New York.
His voice was a curious blend of the accents of the New World
in which he had spent so many years and those of the Scottish
Highlands which were his boyhood's home. It had been sober-
ing to sit under Mackintosh. It was exciting to sit under Baillie.
He was remarkable for his understanding of the intellectual
problems which those who think seriously are bound to encounter, and for a lucidity of exposition which in my experience has never been surpassed. You knew when you listened to
him that he was an honest thinker. No link in the chain of
argument was ever missed and you felt that he was willing, and
indeed determined, to follow wherever the argument might
lead, however inconvenient. A colleague in a neighbouring
classroom, Professor G.T. Thomson, a keen, one might almost
say a besotted, Barthian, hit us over the head, so to speak, with
ex cathedra propositions. To his very great credit he had no
objections to our hitting him back which many of us did with a
will. He was as kind and generous himself as his theological
position was inhospitable and unbending. No greater contrast
to John Baillie could possibly be imagined. Baillie was not a
Barthian but he knew why, and he could tell us. His chair was
that of Divinity, which meant that he was concerned not primarily with the enunciation of the articles of Christian belief
but with their interpretation. He was a man of wide culture. He
was a philosopher as well as a theologian and he could explain
to us why it was important to try to be both at the same time.
The influence of Karl Barth was already powerful in Britain as
in the States and frequently, as will often be the case, those
enamoured of the continental neo-orthodoxy were more
Barthian than Barth. There was and is still much to be learned
from this theological giant. Baillie worked hard to see that we
got the message and showed us why he himself could only

receive it with reservations. A.E. Taylor had awakened my interest in Moral Philosophy. Now Baillie seemed to me to be talking the same language and leading me further on in a field of study I found completely fascinating. I felt more and more at home with his approach and apparently he thought so too. He regarded my examination papers with such approval that I qualified for a travel scholarship to Palestine, as it was still known in 1935. There, in company with a group of fellow students, I spent a most delightful and rewarding summer term, seeing for myself those places with which the Bible had long made me familiar. It was a very happy ending to an unforgettable year.

In my third and last year in New College I might well have become absorbed in the theological studies which I had already found so agreeable and for which I had shown at least some aptitude. It was not to work out that way. I didn't take to any form of riotous living. For that I lacked both the means and any very strong desire. I took instead to the Settlement which New College maintained as a centre of practical student training. I had already been spending a certain amount of time there. Now it began to occupy more than its fair share of my attention.

New College Settlement was situated in the district of Edinburgh known by the incongruous name of the Pleasance. Perhaps by that time it had lost the doubtful distinction it once enjoyed as the most densely populated area in Europe, but it cannot have dropped too low on the list. The Settlement was quite a small building containing club-rooms for the various activities and a residence for the few students involved. A young minister, straight from College, presided over the establishment as Sub-Warden. The Settlement was the province of the student Missionary Association. I had been secretary of the Association and in my third year became President. Rightly or wrongly, most probably wrongly, I felt that the organisation would immediately fall apart without my constant personal participation in its affairs. I proceeded to spend more and more time in the Settlement and less and less time at my books. I still obtained my degree at the end of the day but did so in a most undistinguished manner, greatly to my mother's disappointment, and indeed to my own also. I have never been able to accept the fact – plain, I am sure, to the meanest intelligence – that I cannot do everything I want to do equally well at one and the same time. Perhaps this is a common human failing. It certainly has been mine.

The Settlement no longer exists, but then neither does the Pleasance as I knew it. The dingy tenements have been demolished and replaced by buildings more consistent with the needs and dignity of their occupants. The original inhabitants have long since been transported to new housing areas on the outskirts of the city. A Settlement would no doubt be superfluous now. It was only too necessary in the thirties when unemployment was at its height and dole payments woefully, tragically inadequate for the support of those dependent upon them. There was little enough money available for drink but no wonder that it was so often squandered in the pubs which probably looked like the only bright spot in these drab surroundings. We did our best to make the Settlement another such attraction with our activities for children and young people and their parents. Apart from the Sub-Warden all the helpers were students and therefore part-time. Those who lived in the residence normally did most of the work. I lived at home throughout the three years' College course and only moved in at its conclusion when I was appointed Sub-Warden, serving my Probationer year in this capacity.

My special interest as a student was the Unemployed Men's Club. I shared the leadership with my fellow student Walter Johnston, University goalkeeper. Increasingly my evenings were spent with the men of all ages who came to play billiards or read or talk in the leisure which was all too generously at their disposal. Harry was one of our most regular supporters. I well remember the occasion when he arrived very much the worse for wear and failed in one way or another to conform to the Club's accepted standards of behaviour. Perhaps he sensed that I cast a disapproving look in his direction, although nothing had been said. 'Mister McLuskey,' he said with a look of appeal I have never forgotten, 'every man's entitled to his kick at the ba'.' Indeed he is, but the entitlement was little honoured in the thirties in Scotland. Unemployment took its deadly toll of human dignity. Hundreds of thousands lived on or below the poverty level. Housing conditions in the Pleasance had to be seen to be believed. Homes as often as not consisted of one small room in a wretched building in which the totally inadequate sanitary arrangements were shared by far too many people. Little wonder that those of us who worked and for a brief period lived in such an area longed and prayed for a welfare state in which the legitimate needs of any would be the practical and urgent concern of us all.

The dream is now a reality, achieved as much by the compelling needs of wartime Britain as by the efforts of any one political party, but the ideal social order still continues to elude us. The Pleasance and similar under-privileged areas have long since disappeared but drunkenness is at least as bad in Edinburgh today as it was in the thirties and among young people a good deal worse. It was much safer to walk through the Pleasance even on a Saturday night than it is to wander round the more salubrious localities of our great cities today. Teenage hooligans and violence in all sections of the population are on the increase. The Edinburgh I knew well in the thirties had scarcely any trace of the problem, and even in Glasgow of the same period, depicted so vividly in *No Mean City*, gang warfare was an isolated phenomenon and one with which the authorities knew how to deal effectively. No one wishes for material improvement more fervently than I did as I climbed dark tenement stairs and watched children undernourished and inadequately housed, without shoes or stockings, qualifying for tuberculosis like their parents before them. Tuberculosis has almost entirely disappeared. Vast new housing areas have replaced the old shameful slums. Millions of our senior citizens ought to acknowledge that they have never had it so good, for that is certainly the case. At the same time Britain, sixty years later, once again faces widespread unemployment. The problems of the thirties were very different. Those of the nineties are no less formidable. In some respects they are infinitely more daunting. The quality of our national life has declined as rapidly as material benefits have increased. It is no justification for social inequality and social economic injustice to claim, as I am bound to do, that areas such as the Pleasance in the hungry thirties produced some of the finest men and women I have known. What must be said, and said plainly, is that programmes of social and economic betterment in themselves provide no guarantee of a country fit for heroes, or anyone else for that matter, to live in.

To put it in a nutshell, that was the message which came across to me in different ways as I pursued the subjects of study in New College and in some slight measure shared the circumstances of my friends in the Pleasance. 'Man shall not live by bread alone but by every Word that proceeds from the mouth of God.' Man most certainly will not live without bread. That lesson had been brought home to me forcibly enough well before I made the acquaintance of the Settlement. Indeed I think it was the experience of our family misfortunes which took me there in the first instance. Whatever Christianity might mean, I knew it could mean nothing at all if it had no concern for those in need. At the same time a Christian home and a minister I loved and trusted had taught me that our needs are more than material and that the world will never be put to rights until the men and women in it are enabled to live as God intends they should. The experiences in the Settlement kept me from any theological cloud-cuckoo-land. The men to whom I listened morning after morning in College acquainted me at a deeper level with our human situation. In some measure at least they showed me what is meant by the Word that proceeds from the mouth of God. It involved an understanding of what the Bible in Old and New Testament proclaims. It involved as clear and full an understanding of the person and teaching of Jesus Christ as could be gained from a study of the New Testament and the subsequent history of the Christian Church. It called for an acquaintance with the faiths of the non-Christian world since those who held them were God's children also and made in His image. It called for an understanding of the faith of those who said they had none but in reality gave their vote for the gospel that man needs no supernatural help, even if it exists, and has what it takes in himself to ensure the healing of those ills, national and international, social and economic, to which flesh is heir. The most dyed-in-the-wool humanist would have been hard put to it to emerge unscathed from day to day encounter with men such as H.R. Mackintosh and John Baillie. Each in his own way armed us for the battle we would have to fight as ministers of the Christian Gospel with unbelievers and false believers. They taught us too that first that battle must be waged and won in our own hearts.

The author as Chaplain to the 1st SAS Regiment in 1944.

Service in the woods in enemy-occupied France in 1944. The author stands beside the improvised Communion Table.

With the Black Watch in Germany, 1984

The Manse family in Broughty Ferry in 1953 – Irene, Fraser, Kenneth and Andrew.

Her Majesty Queen Elizabeth the Queen Mother marks the Silver Jubilee of the new building by revisiting St. Columba's of which, as Queen. Her Majesty had laid the foundation stone in 1950. (© Belgrave Press Bureau.)

General Assembly scene, 1983. The author is in the Chair. (© Anne H. Maxwell.)

Dr and Mrs McLuskey with the Lord Mayor of London at the Mansion House.

Malcolm Mackinnon, the tailor responsible for Dr McLuskey's Moderatorial outfit, turned out to be an old SAS companion. The Bible is presented as a token of appreciation.

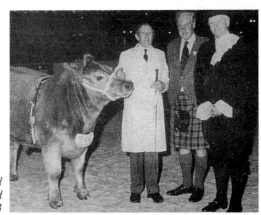

The Moderator meets all sorts on tour! Smithfield Show, December 1983

Visit to Lothian & Borders Police Headquarters, 29th March 1984.

*Her Majesty Queen Elizabeth visits St. Columba's on 21st March 1984 on the occasion
of the Centenary of the move of the Congregation to Pont Street.
(© Uppa Commercial Photographers.)*

Chapter 4

Travelship Scholar in Nazi Germany

The year I spent as resident Sub-Warden at the Settlement was a very happy one and I shall always be grateful for it. Over the years a precious relationship of friendship and trust had been established between the Pleasance residents and the students and young ministers who came to help a little and learn a lot. It was a classroom I was very loth to leave although, as it proved, I was about to enter another no less memorable.

I had been appointed Scottish Secretary of the Student Christian Movement but there was a gap of the spring and summer months before I was due to start. The Principal of New College, Professor William Curtis, proposed that I should spend these months in Germany learning the language and acquainting myself as far as I could with the Church situation there. I was awarded a travel scholarship for this purpose and instructed to report to a small theological college in Wuppertal and to take it from there.

I knew I would be stepping from one world into another. In 1938 Hitler had been in control of Germany for five years. One after another the various citadels of freedom had fallen, in most cases without much of a struggle. Hitler had given the nation a new birth and most of his fellow-countrymen were grateful for it. Unemployment had been tackled and in large measure defeated. New motorways were being constructed. Railway stations were now works of art. Architecture had a new and exciting face. Germany was on its feet and on the march as the never-ending processions of all ages from childhood upwards unceasingly proclaimed. No longer need Germans feel ashamed of their World War One defeat. The horrors of inflation, the paralysis of so-called democracy, lay behind them. They were strong again, well able to reclaim the territories of which they had been deprived. Parts of the Nazi package deal were, of course, distasteful to some. The traditional rights and liberties of the subject had virtually disappeared, but no doubt they would be restored when the emergency had passed. Desperate situations call for desperate measures and so the indoctrination to which all were now exposed, the growing impotence of the judiciary, the dominance of the various military and para-military formations, were all accepted. On balance the Nazi package was what was needed and the less attractive of the contents was a small price to pay. Unless, of course, you happened to be a Jew. Not that the German man in the street was particularly pro-Jew. The country needed cleaning up and some at least of the Jews had been implicated in the rackets Hitler was said to have uncovered. The moral recovery of the nation was priority number one and if Jewish influence had been harmful, and Hitler said it had, then it must be removed before any more damage was done. You did hear of Nazi concentration camps in which Jews and other enemies of the state were herded together but you couldn't and shouldn't believe all that you heard. No doubt many of the horror tales were told to discredit all that Hitler was so valiantly striving to achieve for the beloved Fatherland. In any case this was not the moment to put a foot wrong yourself with Party members watching every move and even your own children ready to report any criticism you might voice or feel of the regime. Heil Hitler!

I believe this sums up the feelings of the majority, whether Church members or not. The Church, however, was to produce an organised opposition to Hitler such as no other section of the community provided. In the Reichstag, in the law courts, in schools, in universities, in the armed forces, Hitler was allowed to have his way. Only in the Church did he meet a courageous and determined minority prepared to resist, if need be to the death.

The story of the German Confessional Church has now been told, notably by the biographers of Dietrich Bonhoeffer. During the months I spent in Nazi Germany I could in some measure watch it being written. It began with Hitler's attempt to form a national Protestant Church to replace the hitherto separate and independent provincial churches. He was himself at least a nominal Roman Catholic and even in his wildest moments of megalomania could hardly expect to displace the Pope. He accepted the fact that the Roman Catholic Church in Germany must be allowed to lead its own life and run its own affairs, always provided it refrained from interference in politics.

Hitler saw his real opportunity in the Protestant sector. Surely a national organisation could be created, led by Nazi sympathisers, to support the state in these realms which were its proper province. The Church was not short of such sympathisers. As the Nazis struggled to gain power a substantial number of Church members had allied themselves with their cause, regarding it as entirely compatible with the Christianity they had now tailored to suit it. Those who felt this way became known as the German Christians. In the view of their critics they were Germans first and Christians second, which meant that in a number of vitally important respects they were not Christians at all. Soon after his accession to power the national Church was formed and after some early struggles Hitler forced his own men into key positions. Thereafter those who could not accept their leadership were compelled to create their own parallel structure which came to be known as the Confessional

Church since it took its stand on the historic confessions of
faith on which the Christian Church is built. It may be said to
have first emerged into the light of day when under the
leadership of Niemoller, Bonhoeffer and others the Emergency
League of Pastors was formed in September 1933. Those sign-
ing pledged themselves to Scripture and the Creeds, to assist
those suffering from Nazi attack such as pastors deprived of
their livings and Jews and others now in great peril, and finally
to repudiate the Aryan Paragraph which made Jewish blood a
disqualification for any post in the Civil Service. This
courageous declaration was followed in May 1934 by the now
famous Synod of Barmen in which the signatories reaffirmed
the constitution of the Federation of the Protestant Churches in
Germany, already recognised by the State, and adopted a
confession of faith prepared by Karl Barth. It was a clear and
public challenge to the German Christians and to a Church
leadership which the Confessional Church could not recognise.

The brave Christian men who then stood up to be counted
did not consider that they were taking political action. They
wished to be loyal to the state and to the Führer. At the same
time they felt compelled to challenge Hitler's men in the
Church leadership and the racist doctrines to which the Nazi
Party and the German Christians were alike committed.
Luther's conception of the separation of Church and State was
basic in their thinking. It enabled them to make their protest on
what they considered legitimate Church grounds while escap-
ing the charge that they were trespassing on grounds properly
the preserve of the State. It was Hitler who was to blame for
crossing the boundary line and failing to remain on the side
where he could hold undisputed sway. Only very gradually and
reluctantly did some of the Confessional churchmen recognise
that Luther's doctrine could be and had been pressed too far.
The claims of Jesus Christ were in fact as totalitarian as those of
the Führer. The writ of the Saviour must run everywhere and it

could not be confined to the realm of religion. In a sense the Nazi dictatorship taught Christians in Germany a necessary and salutory lesson to the effect that Christian discipleship must be exercised everywhere if it is to be exercised authentically anywhere. The death knell of religious isolationism sounded when in due course Dietrich Bonhoeffer made the decision to throw in his lot with the plotters of Hitler's assassination, not just because he was interfering with the Church but because his leadership of the nation could not be tolerated by Christian men. Perhaps to speak of the death knell is to be guilty of exaggeration and wishful thinking. At least one may claim that Bonhoeffer's 'meddling' with politics, his willingness to 'get his hands dirty', as the saying does, signalled a new birth of Christian witness in Germany. A nation doesn't lose its deep-seated characteristics overnight, least of all when it is the night of defeat. Nevertheless there is evidence enough in post-war Germany that political responsibility and political action are being seen as necessary parts of Christian discipleship. If this is so then the Christian Church may claim more than a fair share in the creation of a democratic Germany for which Europe and the world have had so long to wait.

I knew a little of the general situation when around midnight I arrived in Wuppertal. I was met by Pastor Locher, a lecturer in the College and one of the team of ministers in the local Reformed congregation. He informed me that the College had been closed for some time. Members of the Gestapo had sealed the classrooms to ensure that they could no longer be used. A part of the building was still in use as a residence and there was a room reserved for me there. This became my base for the months that followed. The two occupants, apart from the housekeeper, were Pastor Locher himself and a theological student from Hungary. The fact that Gonczy Sandor could speak not a word of English and that I could speak neither Hungarian nor German didn't matter. We became firm friends, communicating with snatches of Latin and Greek and even the odd word of Hebrew thrown in.

Beni Locher, fortunately for me, was a fluent English speaker. Over the weeks that followed he took in hand to fill me in on the position of the Church in Germany as he understood it. I learned that the Confessional Church was not a separate institution but a movement within the established Church, whether Lutheran or Reformed. In the team some pastors might be Confessional sympathisers while others were not. When a known Confessional man was preaching, the Gestapo would be in the congregation writing down what he said. Frequently the preacher would be summoned to Gestapo headquarters and asked to explain his meaning. If the explanation was not considered satisfactory prison or concentration camp could follow and often did. This was happening all over Germany. It had happened to Martin Niemoller in his busy and renowned Berlin parish. It had happened to Paul Schneider in his small country charge in the middle of nowhere. It might happen any day to Pastor Locher or one of his colleagues. Hitler had set the clock back in more ways than one. History was repeating itself. Once again Christian believers were being made to sacrifice liberty and life itself in obedience to their Master. As to this sealed College, I was assured that its work was still proceeding underground. Classes had simply been transferred to the homes of pastors who could be trusted. From time to time the location would be switched and every effort was made to preserve secrecy. While Confessional sympathisers continued to exercise their ministry in an open and above-board manner in the various congregations to which they were attached, it was essential in their view that the training of theological students should be left in the hands of those they could trust. In this way the supply of Confessional pastors would be secured. Underground education for the ministry was proceeding throughout Germany. Dietrich Bonhoeffer himself directed such a Seminary in Finkenwalde.

In due course I was taken to attend the classes where both Pastor Locher and Dr Herman Hesse, Principal of the College when it had officially existed, lectured as they had done before. Neither they nor the students were under any misapprehension as to the risks involved. What they were doing was illegal. It could cost them their liberty and their lives. I reflected how little we had valued our freedom and our opportunities in student life in Edinburgh. I wondered how my fellow students and I would withstand such a test if, remote though the contingency then appeared, a like situation ever developed in Britain.

I took such part as I could in the day to day life of the College but, of course, I was equally concerned to gain at least a working knowledge of the German tongue as quickly as possible. I had been using a Teach Yourself system but now I started to attend instruction at a nearby Berlitz School. Principal Curtis had provided me with an introduction to Dr Paul Humburg who had been a leading figure in the World Alliance of Reformed Churches. He gave me a friendly reception and mentioned that his niece, Irene Calaminus, was on the staff of the Berlitz School and was an excellent teacher. This she certainly proved to be. She was kind enough to consider me an apt pupil but perhaps she was a prejudiced party. After three weeks of daily teaching and learning together we became engaged, to the considerable dismay of our respective families.

Irene was the daughter of a Reformed Pastor in Barmen, which, with Elberfeld, makes up the town of Wuppertal. He was inclined to take a poor view of the young Scot who, as far as he was concerned, was a completely unknown quantity and who was so deficient in the rudimentary arts that he couldn't even speak German properly. He requested me to produce a testimonial from my minister at home with all possible speed. Irene's mother was more forthcoming but I could see she hoped the testimonial would arrive quickly. Irene's three brothers were prepared to give me the benefit of the doubt. Herbert, roughly my own age, was himself a student of theology. The younger ones, Ernst and Ulrich, were students of pharmacy and agriculture respectively. When the testimonial did arrive from my minister Mr Thomson, it was duly translated by Irene and appeared satisfactory. I was accepted and arrangements to celebrate the engagement were put in hand.

Our courtship, brief as it was, had been greatly facilitated by the fact that Irene had a perfect command of English. The Calaminus family had close English connections. There was a link by marriage with the Garret family and the late Douglas Garret, at one time President of the Law Society, had arranged for Irene to spend a year in London as 'house daughter' with Mr and Mrs Clare Logan of Golders Green. The arrangement had been a great success. Clare Logan, completely blind, was a talented musician and broadcaster. The home was a happy one and filled with interesting people. The Logans took Irene to their hearts and she was deeply attached to them. She became Clare's guide and companion on the long walks he loved to take. A lasting friendship developed between the Calaminus and Logan families.

The year in London had been in pleasant contrast to Irene's earlier travels. On leaving High School she had been determined to make languages her special interest. Money was as scarce in German manses as in Scottish. There were three sons to claim their share of higher education and so Irene decided she must work her own educational passage. Her father had a pastor friend in French-speaking Switzerland and he was more than ready to have Irene on an au pair basis. It proved to be a tough assignment and anyone with less grit and determination would have given up and gone home. This was not Irene's way. She had come to perfect her knowledge of French and stayed until she had done so.

She had a natural facility for languages and in addition was a born teacher. She had patience and a conscientious thoroughness combined with a warm and kindly personality and a lively sense of humour. Tall for a woman, she was good-looking rather than sensational. Susceptible as I was to feminine charm, I could have listed a number of girl friends who were superficially more attractive. What bowled me over in so short a time was what Irene was in herself. Her sympathy, her affection, her goodness, kept coming through – most of all in her expressive eyes. Above all she was a giver and as completely unselfish as anyone could be.

The initial suspicion on the part of Pastor and Frau Calaminus had now vanished and I was made one of the family. Musical evenings were very much the order of the day with father at the small organ, Herbert at the piano, Ernst playing the violin and Ulrich the flute. We were often joined by the Biermanns. Mille, who was an aunt by adoption, sang in a rich contralto voice and her husband accompanied. Sometimes the song would be of his composition. In such gracious fashion I was introduced to German home life at its best and discovered just what *Gemütlichkeit* could mean in terms of warm, secure comfort for body and spirit.

Happy as these engagement days were, we didn't lack for problems. Perhaps war would come before we had the chance of making our home together. If war came after we married Irene must face years of separation from her own country and her own people. How would she fare as a German in Scotland? It was easier to ask the question than to find the answers.

Meantime we both had our work to do. I had to see as much of Germany as I could and made a tour of the Rhineland. Heidelberg and Marburg were both on my list and I found that not even Hitler could rob them of their magic. The Nazi presence was obvious enough in Munich and the galleries were dutifully displaying an exhibition of what was disparagingly described as degraded and degrading art, identified, of course, with Jewish artists. At one point my travels took me to

Friedrichshafen on the shores of Lake Constance. My singing teacher in Edinburgh had asked me to look up a family there. The father, Dr Braunfels, had been a Professor of Music in Cologne but being Jewish had been dismissed from his post. Now he was living as unobtrusively as possible in a charming house on the shores of the lake with his wife and daughter. He was a gifted pianist. I can never hear the Appassionata without remembering how he played it as we sat entranced on the verandah. Twenty-five years later I took my two sons and our caravan to Lake Constance. I looked in vain for the house I remembered so well and finally asked at the Post Office counter in Friedrichshafen if the name of Braunfels was still known locally. The assistant at the counter was mystified but an elderly woman standing next to me heard what I was saying and volunteered the information that the daughter was still alive and working in a Roman Catholic Home for old people. I found her there in the office. Neither parent had survived the persecution which intensified as the war continued but somehow or other the daughter had. It was clear that she found some solace in securing for her elderly and infirm patients the happier ending to life denied to her own parents.

My letter of attestation from New College stated that I was visiting Germany both to learn the language and to make any study possible of Christian youth work. Soon after arrival I learned that the German YMCA was still carrying on although its former activities had been drastically reduced. Nothing other than religious instruction was permitted to it. For a movement devoting a large part of its programme to physical and cultural pursuits this was a severe blow. I was particularly anxious to learn how the Student Christian Movement was faring. Until 1933 the German SCM had played a vigorous part in the World Student Christian Federation. I discovered that by 1938 the Movement had been banned but my new Confessional friends were able to put me in touch with the former General Secretary,

Friedrich Von Thadden. He told me that like the Confessional Theological College the Movement still functioned underground. In fact a summer conference would be held in a remote part of Bavaria. If I remember correctly the nearby village was Haslachmuhle. Provided I kept the information to myself and travelled in as inconspicuous manner as possible, I would be welcome to attend. It was the last SCM Conference to be held before the war broke out a year later. There were some thirty students drawn from different university faculties. The programme was similar to any SCM conference in Britain except for the fact that whatever the subject discussion naturally came round to the attitude the Christian should take to the state and, in particular, the Nazi state. By this time my knowledge of the language was sufficient to give me a reasonably accurate idea of what was being said. There appeared to be the same lack of appreciation of the inevitable political implications of the Christian faith which I had so far found to be typical of the Germans I had met. On the other hand, there was a very real awareness of the right of the Church to be free to conduct its own internal life without state interference. Above all, there was abundant and moving evidence of the courage of these young Christian men and women and their determination not to be diverted from what they considered the path of Christian duty. Along with this spirit of deep dedication there was all the gaiety usually associated with student gatherings. Once again I was challenged by the sense of the authentic Christian Church whose members at the beginning and down the centuries and now today were perfectly prepared to tread the path of martyrdom should that be required. I found we were often poles apart when we discussed theology and the relevance of the Christian faith to political and economic issues. I never failed to be humbled by their willingness to pay any price in loyalty to their Master.

I had precisely the same mixture of feelings when on one occasion I attended a day conference for Confessional churchmen in the Ruhr. It was held in Düsseldorf and I received careful instructions for the journey. I was to travel by train to a certain station. On leaving I was to find my way to a side street where I would find my guide examining the contents of a shop window. I must then identify myself and he would do the rest. The conference was called to discuss the legitimacy of Christians taking a certain oath which had just been prescribed for holding any form of public office. Some of the pastors felt that they must as loyal Germans take the oath even if they disapproved of much of the Nazi policy and practice. Others felt that this was now the crunch and that they had come to the point when they must openly declare that the Nazi state was anti-Christ. Biblical questions flowed fast and furious. What had Jesus meant about paying tribute to Caesar? What did Paul mean about the powers that be being ordained by God, and what about 1st Peter, not to mention the prophetic witness of the Old Testament, and much else besides? It was partly a matter of biblical exegesis and theological posture, perhaps even more a matter of temperament. I can't remember how Irene's father voted. I suspect that he favoured taking the oath. He most certainly did not approve of Hitler and would have done anything he could, at risk to himself, to help a Jew or anyone else in trouble. He was a Confessional man in that he took his stand with the Synod of Barmen and rejected utterly everything the German Christians stood for. And yet he wanted to be a loyal German. He believed in his heart of hearts that politics were for politicians, even if they were Nazi politicians. He tried to steer a middle course not because he lacked courage but because he felt that this was what a Christian pastor ought to do. He trod the path of Christian discipleship as he conceived it with the dignity and deliberation characteristic of his conduct of divine worship. When war came he continued the even tenor of his ways and sought to care for his flock in Barmen as he had always done. He was a devoted minister of the Gospel as his forbears had been without a break for seven generations. Neither the Nazis nor World War Two could put him off his stride.

Chapter 5

University Chaplain in Glasgow

The German tour completed and my travel scholarship exhausted, I was due back in Scotland for a family holiday in Nairn before starting work as Scottish Secretary of the Student Christian Movement. Irene found that she could have a holiday too and travelled back with me. The visit to Nairn proved something of a nightmare. It was August 1938 and while we were there Germany invaded Czechoslovakia. It seemed certain that war would be declared. In the event Irene and I decided not to marry at that time. Irene felt that there were some things she must try to do in connection with her job and her home before she took up all her roots. We parted knowing full well that the decision might prove wrong and that the opportunity to marry might be lost for years or forever. When, shortly after, Mr Chamberlain returned in triumph with his Munich piece of paper it seemed we had been wisely guided. Like Britain herself we had been given a little time to prepare.

For the first few months of my SCM work my fiancée was on the wrong side of the Channel. Letters were a great help and the months of separation strengthened our conviction that we were meant to share life together, however awkward, if not impossible, that might presently appear. As it worked out our time apart was shorter than we anticipated. An elderly lady in Edinburgh, a close friend of the family, suggested that Irene came to her as a companion. This was arranged early in 1939 and worked to everyone's satisfaction. We were now clear that Irene was here to stay and whether we were in a position to marry or not we must certainly do so if war seemed imminent. When in August enemy aliens were advised to return to their own countries we immediately arranged for a civil ceremony so that Irene might be legally British. As Scots Law allowed, we took each other as husband and wife in the presence of two witnesses in the office of our solicitor in Edinburgh on 24th August. I see from the certificate that I was then twenty-four and Irene twenty-six. This legal marriage by declaration was duly confirmed by the subsequent issue of the required Sheriff's warrant.

Our good friend Charles Nightingale had retired and his partner William Bell presided at the office ceremony. I shall always remember his graciousness in providing a corsage for Irene in the form of a beautiful rose. By their own request our two witnesses were none other than Miss Burgess, to whom Irene was acting as companion, and my great-uncle Jim who for some years had made his home with us. Both were well into their eighties and both seemed to enjoy their role tremendously.

The marriage service itself was then planned in rather more leisurely fashion and took place one week later in the Pleasance Church on 31st August. Although technically a service of blessing following the legal marriage, both Irene and I regarded this as the beginning of our married life. It meant much to us to enter the new chapter of our lives in the area in which my ministerial apprenticeship had been served, an area of hardship and under-privilege transformed by the kindness and courage of so many of its inhabitants. We were grateful, too, that the service could be conducted by Professor Tindal, Warden of the Settlement, who had been my chief. He had been a friend all through my student days and was one of the kindest and wisest counsellors I have ever known. His familiar hand is still as legible as ever on the back of the official marriage certificate to confirm that the service of blessing took place.

Money was tight but it ran to a couple of days in Edinburgh's Royal British Hotel. It seemed to us the height of luxury and if our honeymoon was brief it could not have been happier. The difficulties we had faced and those we anticipated made our union as husband and wife the more precious. Perhaps the war would still by some fresh miracle be averted. Perhaps the lines to Germany would remain open. Perhaps Irene would still be able to embrace her new life in this country without the total severance of ties with home. Still in something of a post-marital daze I settled the bill on the morning of Sunday 3rd September and we set off to the Berwickshire village of Cockburnspath where I was engaged to conduct morning service. The ancient Austin Ten I still possessed boasted a sunshine roof which was open. At some point on the journey there was the sound of aircraft overhead. I remember that the quite absurd thought crossed my mind that we should take protective action by closing the roof. We arrived in good time for the service. Before it ended war had been declared. The situation we had long discussed and dreaded was now an accomplished fact.

At least to some degree I could understand what this must mean to Irene. She was in a strange country facing separation from her own family for an indefinite period. She could not tell how welcome she would be as a German as the war went on. No one could have been more opposed to Hitler and all he stood for but naturally she loved her own country and could not wish its destruction any more than she could desire the defeat of her newly acquired homeland. She knew she must be prepared to live with a divided loyalty. To add to the problem she had married a young man of not quite twenty-five who had certainly completed his professional training and was in employment at a modest salary but who had virtually no capital whatever. Who could tell either what changes of circumstances the war might bring to him, as to everyone else. As a minister of religion he was in a reserved occupation but who knew how long he would feel able to accept it. Last but not least, where were we going to make our home? In spite of it all I cannot recall any occasion on which Irene seemed to falter in the decision we had taken. She believed, as I did, that God had brought us together and she was fully prepared to leave the future in His hands. This was the way in which she had been taught to look at life from her earliest days. Her two believing parents had shared their own faith with all four of their children and all four had caught the infection of a simple and rock-like trust in the God who comes to meet us in Jesus Christ. Like her parents she had faced the test of Hitler years and knew, far better than I did, what it was to live daily with danger and well-founded fear. I had been especially fortunate in the home of my childhood and youth: now I was to know a companionship no less precious. Irene had already taught me her own language: she now proceeded to show me what married life could be like. I learned at least something of what I shall always owe to her patience and understanding, her courage and her love.

The immediate home problem was quickly solved. Miss Burgess, the dear lady to whom Irene had been companion, offered us accommodation. Then, in much less predictable fashion, my employers, the Church of Scotland Home Board and the SCM, suddenly seconded me to act as Chaplain to the University of Glasgow for a period of six months – this at the request of the then Vice-Chancellor, Principal Sir Hector Hetherington. The Chaplain's residence, fully furnished, went with the job. When the six months were ended the University Court invited me to accept the post of University Chaplain for the normal period of five years. It meant that we could make our home together in a University community in which Irene had already been made warmly welcome. It seemed to me then, as it seems to me now, little less than miraculous.

Until 1930 the University had neither a Chapel nor a Chaplain. When in that year the present lovely Chapel was completed the late Very Reverend Dr Archibald Craig was appointed Chaplain. Dr Craig had served with distinction in the first World War and had subsequently become a convinced pacifist. He was an able scholar and a brilliant speaker and preacher. In addition he had a special gift for winning the confidence and affection of students and staff alike. He was tailor-made for the post of Chaplain. By his own gifts and personality he created the position and filled it with the greatest acceptance until he felt it right to resign at the outbreak of war. It may have been that his pacifist convictions led him to the decision but in any case he had a pressing invitation to become the first General Secretary of the newly formed British Council of Churches. To follow such a man, some thirty years my senior and so incomparably better endowed for the task, was clearly impossible for me in other than a purely temporal sense. On the other hand, I could and did enjoy the goodwill he had won for the appointment. In addition, as I pointed out to my employers, I had a wife while Archie Craig at that time had none and our combined ages totted up to a respectable score. Irene shared the work to the full and friendships formed with students and staff in our home continue to this day.

When he discussed the appointment with me Archie gave me one excellent piece of advice. When in doubt, he said, go to the Principal himself. I soon discovered I could go to no one better. If I know anything today about administration I learned most of it from observing Principal Hetherington as he presided over the complex and complicated organism of the huge and growing University in wartime Glasgow. An hour or more before any office officially opened he was at his desk, profiting from the peace and quiet before the telephones could ring. He was still prepared to be disturbed by his young and inexperienced Chaplain. I tried to keep all such interruptions to the absolute minimum but to know I could always go to the boss with any problem I might have helped enormously. 'You will always find the Principal fair,' Archie had said, and how right he was. In my case he was more than fair and did all he could to encourage me. Both he and Lady Hetherington made Irene and me welcome in their home, as, indeed, did the other dons who lived in the University Square. I remember with special appreciation the kindness of Principal Fulton, Primarius Professor of Divinity, and Mrs Fulton. 'Very appropriate,' he would say after he had heard me preach at the University service. Measured praise, no doubt, but not too discouraging. 'I think you ought to be more vigorous in your delivery,' he said. 'You are a big, strong fellow.' That was the nearest he ever got to saying that I had practically everything to learn about preaching, which was certainly the case.

My most regular critic, as far as preaching was concerned, was the University organist, A.M. Henderson. We met every weekday and normally walked home together after the morning Chapel service. 'A.M.' was then coming near the end of his professional life and so his repertoire as pianist and organist had become more limited, but his standards had certainly not dropped. Everything he did was done to perfection. As one music critic put it: 'A.M. Henderson plays the music most of us think we play.' Both he and his wife took us both to their hearts. This, however, in no way detracted from his determination to set my apprentice feet firmly on the proper preaching path. After each of my sermons I was given a kindly but thorough assessment. The content as a rule passed muster although I remember one occasion when he took issue with me. As the war was now very much on I had thought it right to preach from the text 'Love your enemies'. I think he felt I sounded too dovelike for the times. It reminded me of a similar occasion when an old Scottish worthy had taken his minister to task for preaching on the same text. 'But our Lord said this,' expostulated the minister. 'Aye,' replied his critic, 'and I never thought ony better of Him for that.' Leaving the occasional doctrinal controversy aside, 'A.M.' was mainly concerned with delivery. He recalled a maxim of his German organ teacher. '*Sie müssen Bund spielen,*' he would repeat. Somehow I had to learn to give variety of tone and expression. I have never forgotten his admirable counsels and have tried to profit from them. I need no reminder of our friendship but if I did the gold pencil he gave me when I left for the Army is with me still on my desk.

Support for the Chaplaincy was by no means confined to the Principal and the Divinity Faculty. The Faculty of Medicine and the Faculty of Engineering provided staunch friends. Professor E.P. Cathcart of Physiology never missed the Sunday University service, nor did Professor Howe of Electrical Engineering. Professor Duncan Blair of Anatomy, considerably younger than the others, was outstanding in his concern for the Christian cause in the University. His spiritual home was the 'Wee Frees', that quite small group of Presbyterians who still resolutely refuse to abandon their separate Presbyterian identity. He was an enthusiastic backer also of the University Evangelical Union. Most important of all, he was first and foremost a dedicated Christian man with a heart big and hospitable enough to welcome any and every Christian believer, however differently their faith might find expression. He and his wife Leonie opened their home to us whenever we arrived and became our closest friends although my theological background and tendencies were of so obviously a more liberal nature. I believed and believe still they were nonetheless evangelical and I think Duncan Blair was prepared to agree.

The residents of the University Square were indeed a diverse bunch. One of the University houses, ten times larger than his bachelor needs dictated, housed Professor Mullo Weir, an expert in Semitic languages. Extra powerful lenses suggested that over the years he had just about read himself blind deciphering his recondite scripts. He was far from being a dry as dust scholar. At the annual divinity students' dinner he convulsed the company with a rapid fire comedy turn which would have done credit to Tommy Handley. Willie Tindal was my introduction to Professor Charles Campbell of Logic and Metaphysics. They had been fellow students. Charles Campbell could not commit himself to the orthodox Christian position but had an integrity and a sympathy of mind any Christian believer might covet. Perhaps of all the friends we made in the University community Professor J.D. Mackie and Mrs Mackie meant most of all. It was his gracious way to treat me as an equal. I was never in the least danger of supposing that I was, but the relationship thus extended to me was particularly precious. But that being said, I cannot think of any of my new learned friends and colleagues who failed to accept me as a younger brother or ever implied that I had singularly few qualifications to be there.

Preaching at the University service loomed large among my duties. When Principal Fulton suggested I lacked vigour of delivery he was absolutely right. It was partly due to the fact that from my earliest days I had been extremely nervous in public. As a child I suffered agonies when playing the piano to an audience. I was similarly uncomfortable when as a divinity student I was first let loose in the pulpit. Years passed before I acquired any sense of ease and confidence. Without the Army to teach me I might never have learned at all. Apart from that I had at the outset of my ministry the conviction that it was the Word rather than the preacher that mattered. If I was faithful in delivering the message of Scriptures then in confidence I could leave the rest to God, Whose Word it is. It took a long time to dawn on me that preaching is 'truth through personality' in Phillip Brooks' memorable definition. God can and does use the man as well as the message to bring the message home. No doubt there is a proper tension here. The man can be too prominent so that the true message almost disappears from sight; but I started off at the other extreme. Of course the Chaplain was not expected to preach every Sunday, normally once a month only. On the other Sundays preachers of distinction came by invitation. Some were drawn from the University itself. I have vivid memories of the sermon preached by Arthur J. Gossip, Professor of Christian Homiletics. It was said of him that he spent the whole week laying down the rules of successful preaching to his students and then on Sunday went into the pulpit and broke every one of them – with complete and overwhelming success. On this occasion he took science and religion as his theme. Of a sudden he thrust his scraggy head and neck an unbelievable distance out of the somewhat cramped pulpit. 'What has science done for us?' he almost screamed in his thin reedy voice. 'I'll tell you. It has made us cleverer devils than we were before.'

The University Chapel is not large and so no great congregation was required to make it feel reasonably full. At most the congregation was a token one. In a non-residential University those students and members of staff who were accustomed to worship on Sundays normally went to the congregation to which they belonged. The Chapel attracted the students who lived in University residences or in lodgings nearby. The members of staff who came regularly were those who cared deeply about the University community and the need to set Christian worship at the centre of its life. They were, and no doubt still are, a minority but a richly influential one.

University Prayers were said daily in term at nine o'clock. Here the numbers were normally small but the provision of the daily service, like that of the Chapel itself, was a statement of faith by the University. The Universities which have mushroomed since the war in many cases make no such provision and by the same token make their own very different declaration of faith.

The greater part of my time as Chaplain was occupied with such pastoral care as might be exercised in the circumstances. As a young man at the outset of my ministry I could not expect to be of much service to members of staff so much older and so much more gifted and experienced than myself. I could try to get alongside the students who were only a few years younger. I was given every opportunity to do this. Students could be visited in residences, in their lodgings, in the student unions. The hospitals were helpful in notifying student admissions. The University Training Corps for the three services was working full cock and the Chaplain could share in their activities. The Student International Club was as active and cosmopolitan as ever under the inspiring leadership of Appadurai Aaron and his equally talented wife. The demands of the war effort raised rather than lowered the tempo of University life. If at times I asked myself why like most of my contemporaries I was not in uniform, at least I knew that I had more than a full-time job where I was.

Not that I was totally devoid of uniform either. When I was appointed University Chaplain I joined the local Civil Defence Force. For this I was issued with the statutory equipment including the prescribed dark blue battle dress. As a part-time member of the Forces I was on duty from seven o'clock on Thursday evening to seven o'clock on Friday morning, once a week. Apart from this regular commitment I had to report to our Partick Depot as often as the air raid sirens sounded. I had one University colleague in the Depot, Professor of Botany John Walton, and also a fellow minister, the Reverend W.J. Smith of Claremont Parish.

We were all required to have some knowledge of first aid but my main responsibility was to drive a bus ambulance, an ancient vehicle which had once been a double decker bus but had now been deprived of its upper story. Driving the bus presented no problems. The real test was to start it. This demanded a strong arm indeed as the self-starter, if it had ever functioned, had long since given up the unequal struggle. Once the engine had been coaxed into reluctant life all was well. The only practice outings I recall with real displeasure were those in which we were required to drive with our gas masks on. The discomfort seemed greater than anything the enemy were likely to inflict.

When the expected raids did materialise in March 1941 they were severe enough. Glasgow and neighbouring areas sustained heavy damage and casualties. In the district served by our depot Yarrow's Shipyard received several direct hits, one of which shattered the air raid shelter. It was the test for which we had been training and preparing for two years. Nobody was looking for trouble but I think most of us felt relieved that we were now taking at least some share in the afflictions to which Londoners and others had for so long been exposed. We were privileged to be civilians and in our own homes but now we were under fire too, and even if the experience had its terrifying moments the thought gave some satisfaction.

As far as I was concerned the satisfaction was only partial. I had no doubt that my work in the University was important and that the Home Front with its needs and dangers required to be manned no less than the fighting services. On the other hand, as the 'phoney' war receded into the long distance and the conflict took its ever increasing toll, I felt more and more conscious that I must take some share in the lot of my contemporaries who had left civilian life behind them. I had shared my feelings with Irene often enough and knew I had her full support. To be without her husband in these war years was bad enough for any wife and for Irene as a German it was clearly very much worse. Nevertheless she was determined that I should not work on in the University solely on her account. Somehow or other she would manage to look after herself and Joan, the daughter born to us in December 1942. If I felt I had to go I would go with her blessing.

I was no longer in any doubt and told Principal Hetherington of our decision. He informed me that my appointment as University Chaplain would continue but that I would be granted leave of absence until the war ended. Accepting the advice that I would be more useful to the services in my professional capacity than in any other I proceeded to report to the Army Chaplains' Training Centre in Tidworth on Salisbury Plain in April 1943. The ache in my heart told me that at last I was beginning to share in the experience of those who had made the parting with home and loved ones years ago.

Chapter 6

Wartime Army Chaplain

I have described my short period of Army service in my book *Parachute Padre* (Spa Books). As the years have passed I have been more and more grateful for the experience. If there had to be a war I am glad to have had at least some share in all that it meant for our servicemen. I was of course fortunate that, unlike so many Army Chaplains, I survived intact. Above all I was given the opportunity to form friendships which have enriched life ever since. Comradeship is one of wartime's most precious by-products.

My introduction to service life was both helpful and kindly. During the First World War Army Chaplains were catapulted direct to their place of service totally unaware of what their change of life might demand. Things were managed much better in World War Two. On first enlistment ministers, whatever their denomination, received a three weeks' training designed to equip them, sartorially, physically, mentally and spiritually for their status. The Roman Catholic Church maintained its own initial training centre. Protestant clergy shared the Chaplaincy School at Tidworth on the Salisbury Plain. When I reported there in the spring of 1943 the Warden was the Reverend Frank Woods. He and his colleagues saw to it that we were given some idea of the way that Army lives and moves and has its being and the opportunities given to its

Chaplains. What we now had to learn was how our ministry might most effectively be exercised in its new military setting in the course of a war fought to ensure the survival of our country and the liberties enshrined in its unwritten constitution. Ranked as officers, we were part of the great machine and so had to learn what this involved.

It is sometimes argued that a Minister of Religion would be better able to fulfil his calling in the Services unranked. This appears to be the view taken in the Navy although there the unranked Chaplain is treated for all practical purposes as an officer. In both the Army and the Royal Air Force the Chaplain has officer status and may in due course climb the rank ladder as his experience and responsibilities justify. Rank, however, would never be 'pulled' by any minister who had even the faintest appreciation of his calling. Rank is given so that the Chaplain may be integrated within a system of which it is an indispensable part. It is also given to indicate the recognition by the Services of the importance of the Chaplain's work. Whether or not that work is well done depends not on the nature of the uniform worn but on the character of the man inside. In all the circumstances the uniform is a necessary help and need never be a hindrance. Certainly by the time our instruction in Tidworth had ended we were able to wear it with greater comfort and confidence. When notices of posting arrived we felt certain we would be able to salute our next commanding officer without at the same time knocking our hats off.

In my case posting came as a somewhat unpleasant surprise. When I offered my services as a Chaplain I was assured that there would be a place for me with one of our Scottish Regiments. Perhaps someone, in a manner not unknown in Service life, had blundered but for whatever the reason I was informed that I should report to the Headquarters of the Northern Command at York. From there I was directed to the Headquarters of the South Lincs Sub District in Sleaford. For the months which followed I was no one's padre in particular and everyone's padre in general, provided always that everyone was neither Anglican nor Roman Catholic. In other words I was appointed to minister to the needs of Church of Scotland and other Presbyterian personnel scattered throughout the area, along with those Methodists, Baptists and Congregationalists who were without Chaplains of their own. If the months spent in this peripatetic ministry were in many ways instructive for me as I visited a great variety of Army units, I cannot say they were particularly enjoyable. The winter winds which did their best to blow me off my Army motorcycle were less trying than the sense that I didn't really 'belong' to any of the groups I visited. My welcome was kindly enough as I conducted services, confirmation classes, Padre's Hours, but I was a stranger among strangers. There was a real job to be done and it didn't lack its encouragements but my thoughts often turned to the very different lot of the Regimental Chaplain who is part of the family to which he ministers.

The opportunity was to come to me in a way I could certainly not have anticipated. Opening one day the rather soulless buff envelope which brought Army communications, I learned that there was a need for Chaplains to volunteer for Parachute training if they were young enough and fit enough. I was both and sent off my application which in due course landed me at Hardwick Camp, Chesterfield, the then Depot and School Airborne Forces. Here for some three weeks aspiring and frequently perspiring parachutists received a rigorous physical training course designed to test whether eventually they would prove 'fit to drop'. If in the process we felt the phrase accurately described our condition throughout the course we hoped nevertheless to graduate to the next stage at Ringway, the RAF Parachute Training School, where the actual parachuting began.

In these days when free-fall parachuting is a hobby for young and old alike, our careful introduction to the art may seem unexciting enough. It certainly could not have been more thorough. 'Synthetic' preparation in a specially adapted hangar gradually conditioned us to jump from a height into thin air holding the desired bodily position and then to absorb the impact of the ground when reached. Thanks to the RAF instructors we acquired the necessary, if limited, expertise before we were let loose first on a captive balloon and then on a real live moving plane. More important far than the knowledge they shared with us our instructors imparted their own much needed confidence. I can only speak for myself but I believe most if not all of my jumping group would say the same. The thought of jumping from an aircraft, or a balloon for that matter, as the experience approached had a petrifying effect. Occasionally some trainee refused to go. If most of us did we would give much of the credit to the men who coached us so admirably. Not a few would thank God in addition. After our first jump from an aircraft one of my companions, a particularly tough character you would have said, came running across the field to speak to me as I was preparing to pack my parachute. 'Padre,' he said, 'It was prayer that got me out of that plane.' It was certainly prayer and the power God supplied in response which enabled me, timid soul as I was and am, to meet the demands of the course. Of course the descent by parachute itself, in good weather, is wholly delightful, accentuated by the realisation that your chute has in fact decided to open; but first you have to abandon the security of the plane, a somewhat unnatural proceeding as various parts of one's anatomy are not slow to point out. I not infrequently recall the reply of an American paratrooper, from somewhere in the deep South, when asked how many jumps he had made. 'Ah haven't made no jumps,' he said. 'Ah've bin pushed fifteen times.' A push is indeed required, even if as a rule it has to be supplied from within. When the coveted wings are awarded and worn, the push, whatever its origin, seems well worth while.

The authorities which had been slow enough to respond to my offer to train for parachuting apparently desired to make amends. No sooner had I qualified for my wings than I was ordered to report to an organisation of which, like most other people at the time, I had never heard. It was called the Special Air Service. Now it is a household word, in demand whenever some emergency, brief or prolonged, calls for a combination of courage, imagination, and a complete mastery of military skills. At least I knew where Ayrshire's Darvel was to be found. Here the 1st SAS Regiment was quartered while the 2nd was nearby in Prestwick. French and Belgian Regiments were soon to be added to bring the SAS to Brigade strength. The invasion of France was expected sooner rather than later and for their particular role the SAS was now being prepared.

I was not the only new recruit at Darvel. Additional officers and men were needed for the months ahead. We soon learned the relatively brief history of our new unit. The brain child of Colonel David Stirling, its valiant and dashing founder, it had been born in the desert. The nature and terrain of the North African war lent themselves to raiding groups, whether sea-borne or land-borne or air-borne. With his own hand-picked Commando-trained band of volunteers, Colonel David raided enemy airfields and in general wrought havoc at points where no British troops were supposed to be. The young SAS had established itself as a force to be reckoned with. When the conflict moved to Sicily and Italy it made its equally memorable contribution. Now, as the 1st and 2nd SAS Regiments, it stood ready to play its part in the liberation of Europe.

Soon after I arrived in Darvel the 2nd acquired its own Chaplain, as did the French and Belgians. I was thus enabled to stay with the 1st as I very much wanted to do. I might well have found my position embarrassing. I was surrounded by the young veterans of the North Africa, Sicily and Italy campaigns, in very many cases decorated for their gallantry. Our Commanding Officer, Lt. Colonel Blair Mayne, DSO and Bar, was already a legend. As a padre come so very lately to the scene of active service, how could I hope to be one of them? In fact from the moment I arrived I felt that I was – not by any right of my own but simply because both officers and men welcomed me as if it were the most natural thing in the world to do and offered me their friendship and their trust. Both have continued and strengthened with the years. There is nothing I value more.

I soon learned, at least in outline, what the role of the Regiment would be when the Invasion was launched. We were divided into four operational Squadrons, A,B,C and D, each one hundred strong. Each Squadron was to be given an area in France into which it would parachute and then engage in such tasks of sabotage and ambush as the situation demanded. Continued operations behind the enemy lines demanded regular supplies of ammunition, petrol, jeeps, food and reinforcements and these the RAF undertook to drop as required. Radio links with the home base were the responsibility of 'Phantom', the special Signals Regiment equipped for our somewhat unorthodox warfare.

Shortly before the massive attacks were launched on the French coast small patrols from the Squadrons took off from our sealed camp at Fairford. On 21st June the main body of A Squadron was to be flown to its area in the Nièvre, a hilly, wooded area in central France. The Regimental Medical Officer, Michael McCready, was to go with them. I applied for permission to be taken also and this was granted. Some forty-nine years later the memory of our departure is vivid still. The hamper containing my 'Church' was to be dropped with me. It contained a silk altar cloth dyed maroon, bearing the Regimental emblem, a winged dagger. I had an oak cross, made in sections to meet transport requirements. There were hymn-books, copies of the New Testament (Service edition), and copies of a Day Book of Prayer. I had added a few books for light and general reading, should opportunity be given. My airborne Communion set found a place in the kit-bag along with a lightweight all-weather sleeping bag, rations for fourteen days, maps, and as much spare clothing as could be crammed in. Incidentally we all jumped in uniform as 'regulars', although Hitler ordered that if we were captured we should be treated as irregulars and forfeit the normal prisoner-of-war privileges. He proved as good and as bad as his word. Our rucksacks which would carry our belongings in due course were attached to our kit-bags which in turn were strapped to one leg when we jumped and then played out to hang beneath us and hit the deck first when we landed. Providentially, as it later proved, I noticed at the last moment that I had failed to pack my jack-knife and slipped it into the pocket of my jumping smock.

A converted Stirling bomber was our transport and there were sixteen of us for 'delivery'. The journey took three and a half hours. If things had gone according to plan we would have jumped in two 'sticks' of eight, the plane making two runs over the dropping-zone where an advance party would be installed, we hoped, to welcome us. It was not to prove so simple. Enemy fighters had been reported and the pilot decided he must dump his load as speedily as possible. This meant that we were all hardly likely to land on the correct spot. Anyway when the green light shone, number one, Captain Roy Bradford, was off and the rest of us followed in as quick succession as possible. Not quick enough however as far as I was concerned. I landed, well beyond the appointed dropping zone, in a dense forest and found myself suspended by my parachute harness from a tree. I couldn't see my height above the ground but, finding my jack-knife providentially within reach and starting to cut myself free, I found the height was considerable. I landed, head first, with such force as deprived me, for some considerable time, of any further interest in the proceedings.

The ground must have been particularly sympathetic or my head unusually tough because, as I hope you, dear reader, will agree, I have shown no signs of subsequent derangement.

My luck continued to hold. I was discovered, still somewhat the worse for wear, by Trooper Micky Flynn who had jumped immediately after me. He, sensible chap, had made a perfect landing. Fortified by his company we set off to find our scattered companions and the Reception Committee. They were there all right and accompanied by a group of the local Maquis who had considerately supplied a large red coach, 'won' in a recent skirmish with the German occupying forces. In much greater comfort than we could have anticipated we were driven to the Headquarters of the Maquis force, supplied *en route* with the vin rouge of the country, bread and boiled eggs. If these were to be the hardships of the expedition we felt we could endure them cheerfully.

I was now in my 'parish' although before many days had passed I wondered how long my unusual incumbency would survive. Taking leave of the hospitable *maquisards* we set off in our requisitioned transport to the camp Major Fraser had established in the woods near the village of Chaleaux. We had landed in France on a Thursday morning and when Sunday came we had our first Service together. My pannier had been recovered from the parachutage. Another was added and we had a Communion Table, clothed with the Cloth and adorned by the Cross. We numbered about thirty and all attended. We were our own organ and choir. Our simple act of worship seemed the natural thing to do. We wanted to give thanks for our preservation thus far. We wanted to commend our operations, our loved ones and ourselves to God's care and keeping. Few of those present were accustomed to regular Sunday worship but all, I am sure, welcomed the opportunity to wait on

God together so that we might find His strength for others and for ourselves. We were engaged in a task on which we believed we could ask His blessing. We sought no selfish advantage for ourselves or our allies. Our aim was the liberation of our fellow men from a hideous tyranny and the preservation of those freedoms upon which any life worth the name must depend. Already the enterprise had taken its terrible toll of friend and foe alike on the invasion beaches. Our fellow members of the SAS, in their scattered areas throughout France, had already sustained their first casualties as we had yet to learn. We were under no illusions as to the risk we ran ourselves. But it was not fear only which prompted our act of worship in those for whom it was an unusual proceeding. Since God has made us for Himself our hearts must be restless until they rest in Him. The defences we so often contrive, the obstructions for which the Churches themselves must share responsibility, were for the moment swept away as we stood together on the threshold of our adventure. We knew our need of one another and our hearts spoke of a deeper need which neither we nor our comrades could supply.

Of course I was due to have my leg pulled in a big way. 'That's what comes of having a service, Padre,' they said to me as before the day ended sounds of firing broke the Sabbath peace. For the first time I saw my morning congregation in action. Each man knew what to do and without unnecessary delay or apparent excitement proceeded to do it. The Medical Officer had his own Aid Post and there I waited with him for the outcome of the engagement. It was not one we would have sought. It was not the object of the exercise to fight pitched battles with forces which would normally far outnumber our own. On this occasion however we had no alternative but to hold our position until we could move to a better one. In the process our Sergeant-Major, Reg Seekings, was hit in the head. I cannot forget the first and last surgical operation at which I assisted, however inexpertly. The bullet lodged deeply at the base of the skull and could not be removed, but Reg, as one would expect, took it in his powerful stride and in no time at all resumed normal operations.

The attack, from whatever quarter, was later abandoned. Perhaps the Germans assumed that the nearby Maquis, against whom it had been directed, had been effectively routed, as indeed it had. At daybreak Major Fraser decided we should move deeper into the forest. This we did, lumbered with as much kit as we could carry and being forced to leave the rest concealed as well as possible, hopefully for collection later. We are unlikely to forget that morning's march, in pouring rain, but there was nothing for it but to keep going until we reached a position in which we could feel reasonably secure. This was only a temporary respite. When darkness fell we reformed our convoy and embarked on what seemed a never-ending trek through the forest to reach the little village of Mazignen. Bill Fraser had already reconnoitred the area and knew exactly where he wished to establish his headquarters. It proved to be a wise decision as far as the enemy was concerned. There were no alarms. In other respects the three weeks I spent there could hardly have been more uncomfortable. It rained and rained and rained. The weather was so bad that the planes on which we were relying for supplies failed to arrive. Strong German forces had dispersed the Maquis in the area and there were few farm houses within reach. Our own rations, supplemented by return visits to our original camp site, were soon exhausted. For the first time in my life I began to learn what it felt like to be hungry. But the planes came eventually, three of them. In addition to the other precious supplies each plane carried a jeep and, almost unbelievably, each jeep was eventually extricated from its point of impact and roared into life. There was petrol, ammunition, rations, cigarettes and, last but by no means least, mail. Tony Trower, an officer from HQ Squadron, also came fluttering down amid the other items, so we had first hand news of the Regiment also. Our first three weeks in France had a very happy ending.

The first 'drop' meant that A Squadron could now divide for its appointed tasks. Alec Muirhead with his troop was established at Ouroux. Johnny Wiseman now set off with his men for a location south-west of Dijon. Troop Three, under Roy Bradford, meantime remained at the base camp where our third jeep was required. Civilian transport was quickly acquired and soon a colourful collection of Renaults, Peugeots and Citroëns clustered round the camp. I was allowed to make my own choice of a vehicle and selected what looked like a brand new Renault, about the size of a Morris Minor. I judged it would just about accommodate my travelling companion, Harry Wilson, appointed as my batman, but known by the weapons never far from his reach as the Padre's Private Army. Larger vehicles would have given two six-footers-plus more comfort but I hoped the little Renault would compensate in reliability for what it lacked in space, and this is certainly did. Although Harry and I had a jeep for our own use in the later stages of the campaign, the Renault served us well on our parish rounds.

As the map shows, these had to be extensive if I was to keep in touch with my scattered parishioners. They were continually on the move as duties demanded but at least they had their bases to which they returned and where I could plan to visit them. Upon occasion, when greater numbers were involved and the doctor accompanied them, I could go too as an additional driver and first aid man. I was never armed, although you might say Harry was sufficiently equipped for two. I wasn't there as a fighting man but had my own job to do. I was the better able to do it because so far as possible I was sharing the life my 'flock' had to lead. I was the better able to do it because, unarmed, I represented the peace which the men knew well is God's will for a warring world. The operations undertaken, to sabotage

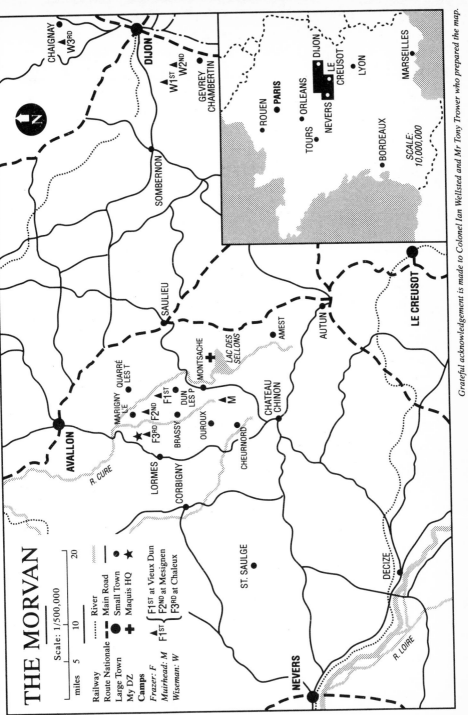

THE MORVAN

Scale: 1/500,000

miles 5   10   20

Railway .... River
Route Nationale ▬▬ Main Road
Large Town ● Small Town
My DZ ★ Maquis HQ ✚

Camps
Frazer: F   F1ST {F1ST at Vieux Dun
Muirhead: M   F2ND at Mesignen
Wiseman: W   F3RD at Chaleux

N

CHAIGNAY ● W3RD
DIJON
W1ST W2ND
GEVREY CHAMBERTIN ●
SOMBERNON
SAULIEU
MONTSACHE ✚
LAC DES SELLONS
AMEST ●
AUTUN
LE CREUSOT ●
AVALLON
R. CURE
MARIGNY LE ● QUARRÉ LES T
F3RD F2ND F1ST
BRASSY DUN LES P
OUROUX M
CHEURNORD
CHATEAU CHINON
LORMES
CORBIGNY
ST. SAULGE
DECIZE
R. LOIRE
NEVERS

ROUEN ●
PARIS ●
ORLEANS ●
TOURS ●
NEVERS
DIJON
LE CREUSOT
LYON ●
BORDEAUX ●
MARSEILLES ●

SCALE: 10,000,000

Grateful acknowledgement is made to Colonel Ian Wellsted and Mr Tony Trower who prepared the map.

vital installations or to ambush the enemy, were in the interests of winning that peace from which all, not least the citizens of Nazi Germany, might benefit. It seemed no other way was open to secure it.

In this context I visited the scattered groups, some larger, some smaller. It was usually possible to conduct worship, either on a Sunday or a weekday. When there were communicants in the camp, whatever their denomination, I could celebrate the Sacrament. For me, as I believe also for those who shared in them, these short, informal services will remain especially precious. Services apart, the normal duties of the ministry found their place. Visitation of 'the flock' went on continually as we lived and ate and drank and travelled together. There were always the casualties to be called on. In some cases the victims of accident or engagement with the enemy were cared for in improvised Maquis hospitals, well served by a brilliant French doctor under the assumed name of Martel, who had joined the Resistance. Within an area of approximately one hundred square miles Harry and I were constantly on the move, doing our best to spend at least some time with every group within our reach. The life we led together made it easy for me to pray with and for my companions and hard for me to say anything concerning the Christian faith of which I was not myself utterly convinced. In a setting which could not have been more abnormal I found opportunities to exercise my calling as great as I have ever known.

As it proved, A Squadron was exceptionally fortunate. B Squadron, under John Tonkin, operated in Deux-sevrès and Vienne. Their exact location became known to the Gestapo Headquarters in Poitiers and their camp of forty-one men was surrounded. Seven managed to escape, three were wounded and Lieutenant Stephens was killed. The remaining thirty were taken captive and, despite Geneva Conventions, were shot. This was later established when their burial ground was discovered by chance. Some thirty years later I visited the area with a group of their former comrades to take part in the dedication of a memorial plinth. The forest swarmed with local inhabitants. School children were there to lay wreaths, the French Airborne Forces provided free-fall displays. It was one of many proofs that the cost of their liberation has not been forgotten by the French.

D Squadron was in trouble too. They had dropped in the Forest of Fontainebleau. The first party to drop, under Pat Garstin, found that their arrival plans had become known. Three men managed to escape. Lieutenant Wiehe was severely wounded and spent the rest of the war in hospital. Those captured eventually suffered the fate of their comrades in B and were shot in defiance of the rules of war.

Only later were we aware of the fate suffered by so many of our friends in other areas but we did know the risks which were involved. In some of our hideaway camps we felt more secure than in others but everywhere we had to be constantly alert. Whenever possible we used the forest tracks and roads on which we were least likely to confront forces greater than our own. Not all the members of A Squadron managed to avoid these encounters. One of our finest officers, Roy Bradford, died as a result.

Only a fool could have been unconcerned by the dangers which were our daily and nightly companions. I can only say that fears, when they visited my own heart, were never disabling. A more constant visitant was the yearning for the wife I had left behind, in greater loneliness than most. To add to her anxieties for her own family in Germany, our dearly beloved daughter Joan had died from cerebral meningitis before I left for France. Homesickness, which had plagued my boyhood days, returned with added strength. But there was the thrill of our Robin Hood existence, the precious friendships of my companions, the excitements of the enterprise, and the daily surprises, whether pleasant or unpleasant. For longer or shorter spells we would enjoy the company of those intrepid men and women who, under the direction of Special Operations Executive, happened to be in one of our areas. From time to time there would be the hectic activity of a supply drop in the middle of the night of which every evidence had to be removed before morning came.

Just how much such supplies could cost came home to us when two aircraft, one British and one American, crashed in the forest near one of our detachments. All the crew had died in their positions. We were able to bury the American airmen ourselves. How glad I was to be at hand to conduct the service for those men who had died so far from their own homes to bring aid to captive France. The British plane, a Halifax, was clearly seen from the road leading to the village of Mazignen. The Mayor had to report its presence to the Germans who arrived in due course and buried the airmen at the nearby cemetery of Marigny L'Église. A week or so later I went to the cemetery with a section of our men to conduct a service of commemoration. I think every man, woman and child in the village must have been there. Years later we received photographs showing the permanent memorial the villagers had raised to the crew.

At the beginning of September the decision was taken to replace A with C squadron. By this time the centre of France was sufficiently clear of German troops to allow the four troops to drive rather than parachute to their areas of operation. Two of them, commanded by Captain Roy Close and Captain Jim Iredale respectively, arrived at Mazignen to relieve Bill Fraser. He had assembled his entire Squadron there for the two days' drive to Auxerre, now in American hands. The column covered half a mile and was dominated by the enormous German troop-carriers on loan from the Maquis Jean. Requisitioned cars mingled with jeeps and the whole scene was one of pleasantly organised confusion. It was a relief to see our casualties at long last heading for home. If all went well 'A' should be home again and on leave within a week. Now for the first time since I had written my parting note to Irene at Fairford, I could send a letter home. It felt almost as good as going home myself.

'C' supplied fighting patrols to escort the convoy to the Allied lines and all went well. Thereafter operations in our area recommenced. They occupied a relatively short space of time since by the end of September the last remaining Germans had been cleared from the centre of France. 'C' most certainly did its efficient best to speed their departure. We had news that Captain Harrison, to the north-east, had suffered casualties, of which he was one. Lieutenant Monty Goddard had been killed in the course of a gallant attack on a German convoy, soon after arrival. Captain Pete Davies reported a highly successful engagement with an immense German convoy near Cosne. Under its commander, Major Tony Marsh, 'C' gave a very good account of itself.

An indication of the extent to which Allied air power now ruled the skies was the parachutage we were able to receive during one afternoon in broad daylight. It felt like a demonstration drop in Tatton Park as the Halifaxes and Stirlings flew overhead and the multi-coloured chutes developed. It was clear that our guerilla days were soon to end. Within a week thereafter we were packing up for home.

Soon after we had arrived in France the neighbouring market town of Dun-les-Places, suspected of Maquis collaboration, was raided by the Germans and burnt to the ground. As many young men as could be found were lined up in front of the Parish Church and shot along with the priest. In the summer of 1987, with former members of the 1st SAS, I revisited Dun-les-Places to share in the annual Commemoration of the tragedy. Monsieur Mitterand, who had formerly been the Deputé for Château Chinon and had himself served in the Resistance, was the Guest of Honour. How warmly we were welcomed and what a joy it was to find two of the Maquis leaders with whom we had worked still, like ourselves, alive and well. The time we had spent in France, less than six months, had by its very nature 'thirled' us, as we say in Scotland, to the land and people as indeed it had 'thirled' land and people to us. In all the circumstances it is not surprising that so short a period came to form such a large and abiding part of our lives.

It must be said that but for the friendship and loyalty of the French our mission would have been doomed from the outset. It would have been only too easy for the locals to give away our positions to the Germans. This they consistently refused to do. In addition, at great risk to themselves, they went out of their way to help us. Little wonder that like so many others I shall always feel that France is a second home.

I can't recall in any detail the leave we were granted on our return from France but I do remember very well one strange feature. I felt impatient to get back to the Regiment. I was grateful for every hour at home with Irene but at the same time was consumed by the thought that it was essential for me to be back at my post. Considering how well the war effort and my Regiment had fared until my belated appearance on the scene my concern was clearly absurd. Perhaps the nervous strain of even such a short time behind the enemy lines was making itself felt in an over anxiety to 'drive to the sound of the guns'.

I might have settled to my leave with greater composure had I been able to visualise the campaign in which we were shortly to share. It was as conventional and, for me, frequently as tedious as our time in France had been unorthodox and almost invariably exciting. We were issued with armoured jeeps and posted as a unit to the 2nd Army which we were to accompany as it took its conquering way through Belgium, Holland and Germany. Our role was to reconnoitre for the armoured cars which led the advance. This meant there was plenty of action both before the Rhine was crossed and afterwards as Germany itself was invaded. In the nature of things the Regiment was more dispersed than ever. The sense of a close-knit fellowship was inevitably lost and my work as Chaplain grew correspondingly difficult. It was a particularly hard winter and my recollections of the dreary flatness of the Low Countries are as uncomfortable as they are vague.

Of course there were bright spots. Like most other members of the Allied Forces, we received a rapturous welcome in Brussels. Along with several of my comrades I was adopted by the family of Monsieur Achille de Jonghe, a wealthy manufacturer, who entertained us with lavish hospitality in his home. Brussels, too, boasted a splendid officers' club where leisure hours could be spent in comfort. When we moved out into less attractive territory we had a welcome no less kindly from the inhabitants who had suffered so terribly under German occupation. As the war advanced and pressure on the Germans increased, their meagre rations were further reduced. A couple with whom I was billeted just inside the Dutch border showed me the apples left in their loft which at times were all that stood between them and starvation. The rations we all enjoyed in Britain, even when convoys were going down and our difficulties were at their height, were princely fare in comparison with the privations the Dutch endured.

It was a new experience for me to see a great Army massed for attack. The narrow cobbled roads were alive with every form of transport. Snow and ice formed additional hazards. The volume of traffic could be as dangerous to life and limb as enemy action. Harry and I needed all our skill as we tried to disentangle ourselves from the endless convoys and keep the jeep intact.

The battle for the Rhine crossing was over before I got there but the evidence abounded. Clearing up operations had not yet begun and men still lay where they had fallen. The cattle and horses unlucky enough to be in the line of fire seemed specially grotesque. The horror of war hit us with a new force.

The more deeply we penetrated German soil the more tragic the conflict appeared. Nothing I had seen of the results of bombing prepared me for the devastation we now encountered. Towns had been obliterated without one landmark left. The plight of such inhabitants as remained was pathetic beyond words. As a Chaplain and a German speaker I acted as an unofficial public relations officer so far as the non-fraternisation policy permitted. There was an endless list of requests for permission of one kind or another and endless requests for help, usually beyond our power to give. Constantly there was the temptation to loot, and for some of our men at least it was too strong to resist. Where houses and shops and factories had been abandoned I suppose they thought the goods were going abegging. If they didn't help themselves somebody else would. And weren't the Germans to blame for it all anyway? Look what they'd done to London and Coventry. Look what they'd done to our own men captured in France. It was understandable, no doubt, but no less saddening. The dangers of the campaign as a guerilla minority in France had seemed to bring out the best in almost everyone. Now, as a tiny part of a mighty force which we knew would soon have Germany at its mercy, the quality of our soldiering, the quality of our living was menaced as never before.

As pathfinders for the armoured cars we reached Lübeck on the Baltic ahead of the main body of troops, and, more important still, ahead of the Russians. One of our Squadrons went on to Kiel and thereafter we hoped to be in Denmark. Two of our officers were Danes and had promised to show us the sights. Just at this point the Germans surrendered and we were spared what to me at least would have been the painful experience of settling down to occupy this shattered land. It was not known whether or not the very considerable German forces in Norway would surrender too and the decision was taken to fly over the First Airborne Division to garrison the country. The SAS were included in the order. To my immense relief we left Germany there and then although my own departure was more leisurely. I routed myself home via the Rhineland, determined to find out what news I could of Irene's family.

Of her parents and her brothers Herbert and Ernst we had heard very little. Herbert, we knew, had served as an officer in Germany while Ernst had been a warrant officer on the Russian front. While still in Glasgow we had undertaken an unexpected journey to Wick to see the youngest boy, Ulrich. He had trained as a pilot. On his very first flight on a bombing mission to England his plane had been shot down and he was captured. We were notified of this through the Red Cross and allowed to visit him in his Prisoner of War Camp. Soon after we saw him he was transferred to Canada and there spent the rest of the war comfortably enough as a lumberjack.

I arrived in Wuppertal to find large areas of the town unrecognisable, including the gracious church square in which Irene's parents lived. I sought out her oldest friend whose home was still intact and learned the news. In the last allied raid of the war the vicarage had received a direct hit. Pastor and Frau Calaminus with their daughter-in-law, Herbert's wife, and her three young children had all died instantly. Herbert and Ernst had both survived although Ernst had been severely wounded. Such was the news I carried home. It came at a particularly trying time for Irene. Our second child was on the way. It had been impossible for the German grandparents to see Joan and she had hoped so much that at least they would meet their second grandchild. Irene accepted the situation in her usual patient way, without the least trace of self-pity. We thanked God that the brothers had all three come through the war and that for the parents the hardships of an occupied country were over. We thought especially of Herbert whose loss had been so severe. We knew our family tribulations were a very tiny part of the vast sum of human suffering the war continued to amass.

The months the unit spent in Norway were unexpectedly carefree. The Germans decided to make no resistance and were duly put in the bag like their comrades elsewhere. Their stores of food and drink were at our disposal and delicacies I had never before tasted became the order of the day. Smoked salmon and wine of like quality were soon taken for granted. To add to our luxury in Bergen, where the greater part of the unit was stationed, we were quartered in blocks of modern flats. Bergen can be as wet as Manchester or Greenock but the summer of 1945 elected to be perfect. We could not have asked for a more perfect setting to celebrate the end of the German war.

Some of our Squadron sections were in Oslo and others in Stavanger so I had the excuse to travel and see something of the beauties of the country. My most unforgettable experience was to sail up the Sogne Fjord on a moonlight night so breathtakingly lovely that it was impossible to go to bed.

There were occasional difficulties with the Norwegians, many of whom had put up a brave resistance to German occupation. They were too independent wholly to enjoy the processes of liberation. Tension was most acute when the local ladies transferred their affections to the new arrivals. On the whole we were well received and certainly in Bergen enjoyed most generous hospitality and were made welcome in many a home.

My time in Norway was broken in very happy fashion. While I was there our second child, Kenneth, arrived in Edinburgh and Colonel Paddy granted me special 'paternity' leave.

Had the war with Japan gone on longer we would have found ourselves in Asia. A number of plans were discussed for the deployment of the SAS Brigade at some strategic point, perhaps on the borders of India and China. Before such plans could be finalised the war was over and demobilisation had begun.

The University of Glasgow had applied for my release but there was still one task which I very much wanted to undertake.

When we left for France we were able to give our next of kin only the haziest idea of where we were going and what we hoped to do. In the case of those who were killed the relatives were waiting anxiously for as much information as we could give them. With the Colonel's approval and frequently with the aid of his Humber staff car, I covered many hundreds of miles to meet wives and parents and give them some idea of the circumstances in which their husbands and sons had died. Where meetings were impossible I wrote as fully as I could, but letters are a poor substitute for question and answer face to face.

Chapter 7

Peacetime Army Chaplain

So it's over:
The hours on the barrack square,
The sergeant's voice, the trumpet's blare:
The chafing pack and the helmet's heat,
The aching limbs, the blistered feet:
The heartache when the leave is ended,
The fear and the excitement blended:
The bark and thud and scream of the fight,
Weary discomfort day and night:
The thrill of sights and places strange,
The freedom, romance, the power to range
The wide world o'er, incognito.

So it's over.
You bear us all away
To the home we left, to a fairer day.

And our hearts are heavy when we thought to be glad,
We're afraid of the future within our grasp.

The world war built is the world we knew,
War has given us comrades true.

Where do you bear us, troopship home?
To the homes we knew, to a fairer day?

The problems of returning servicemen and their families, after in many cases six years or more of separation, must have been formidable indeed. My own period of service was comparatively short but even for me resettlement was not without difficulty. I was fortunate to have work to which to return as I was still on the University staff. There was nothing but joy in the reunion with Irene and young Kenneth. My Chaplaincy duties could not have been more congenial but they were soon to be ended: my contract had only eighteen months to run. When in due course it expired I was loth to go. I was much comforted by a talk with Ernest Bullock, the then Professor of Music in the University. I confided my unwillingness to give up my post. 'You won't regret it,' he said. 'When I resigned as Organist and Choirmaster in Westminster Abbey to come here my friends said I was crazy. I didn't agree. A change forces us out of our grooves. A change compels us to rethink our work. A change at the right time is an essential shot in the arm.'

I could see the point, but it was just here that my particular resettlement problem revealed itself. I felt a strong disinclination to undertake the work of the parish ministry for which I had been specially trained. After the freedom and adventure of my brief spell with the SAS, I felt I would be completely stifled by the conventional parish set-up. I thought of probation work or the prison service. None of the doors which appeared of any interest opened. Then out of the blue came an invitation to return to the Army. Thanks to the close friendship between the then Chaplain General, Frederick Llewellyn Hughes and Field Marshall Montgomery, the Army Chaplains Department for the first time in its life was presented with a permanent Depot and Training Centre. By great good fortune and no doubt the exertion of pressure by 'Monty', this was none other than Bagshot Park, Surrey, the former home of the Duke of Connaught. No setting could have been more delightful. It is difficult to believe that despite the Army cut-downs it still survives.

The house had just been acquired and the first Warden, the
Reverend Alan Gibson, had been appointed. It was assumed
that the Warden, like the Chaplain General in those days, must
be Church of England. It was felt desirable that periodically at
least the second in command, the Sub-Warden, should be
Church of Scotland, and this was the appointment I was invited
to accept. The offer carried with it a regular commission so that
if things worked out that way I might remain in the Army for
most of my working life. By the autumn of 1947 we were
established in the stables flat of the stately home, now desig-
nated as an officer's quarter. If the flat itself left something to be
desired, certainly the park with its rhododendrons and azaleas
and the gracious house itself more than compensated.

It was exciting to be in at the birth of a totally new venture.
Never before in peace time had the Chaplains had their own
depot and training centre. Chaplaincy-training had proceeded at
Tidworth during the war and I had myself benefited greatly
from the introduction thus provided to the Chaplain's work.
There was a chance now to incorporate all that was most useful
in the wartime courses in a curriculum designed for the very
different circumstances of the immediate post-war era. It was a
stimulating exercise to join with Alan Gibson and the Chaplain
General in the construction of a course lasting three weeks
which would effectively introduce a newcomer to the way the
Army worked and indicate the very considerable opportunities
offered to the chaplain. Lectures were given by experienced
Chaplains and by representatives of the different branches of
service. Chaplains in training learned of the kindred activities of
the RAMC and the Army Education Corps. They took at least
a cursory glance at the methods adopted by the Army for its
own administration and were taught how the Army chooses to
write its letters. Our resident Quartermaster, Major Pearn, was
an old soldier whose whole life had been spent in the service.
The mysteries of Army forms, Army Council Instructions and

Army Orders presented no problems for him and he proved an apt teacher. After the course had been constructed my special responsibility was to lecture on our opportunities for Christian education in the Padre's Hours and at other times. This at least taught me a great deal, as did the attempt to provide padres with an outline teaching syllabus for these Hours. The composition and revision of such aids occupied a major portion of my time and energy in my three years at Bagshot Park.

Provision for the needs of Chaplains in initial training and retreats was only part of our responsibilities. Equally important was the creation and conduct of Christian Leadership courses for all levels of serving soldiers. Here again we could not claim to be breaking completely new ground. Such courses had been held during the war with very great success in Europe and the Middle East. Now for the first time we had a permanent and splendidly equipped centre for the purpose and could embark on a rather more ambitious programme.

The courses with which I was concerned were run on an interdenominational basis. Roman Catholic visitors were excluded, not by our wish, but simply through the circumstance that the Roman Catholic Church maintains its own separate Chaplains' Branch and so makes separate provision for its adherents. Otherwise Church of England, Church of Scotland and Free Churches all mixed happily together. One of the great merits of service life is the creation of comradeship which frequently transcends divisions perpetuated by the denominationalism which conceals rather than reveals the true nature of the Christian Church.

If we successfully mixed the churches, we had to admit defeat when it came to rank. There were courses for Other Ranks, for Officers and for Senior Officers. In my experience this division worked quite well and led to that degree of homogeneity on each course which certainly advantaged teaching. Our course lasted a week. As with the Chaplains' Training course, there was opportunity for common worship morning and evening in the House Chapel, now succeeded by one purpose-built and well worthy of its function. Lectures and discussion, for which we divided into groups, formed the basis of the course, but in addition we made good use of films and film strips as does the Army in its general training programme. We tried to give some kind of introduction to Christian worship, to prayer and Bible reading. The ecumenical movement loomed large, as did consideration of Christian vocation designed to break down the barriers between the so-called sacred and secular. Those who came were volunteers in most cases and it did not appear that they had chosen the courses simply as a soft option. Interest was normally keen and a real sense of community developed throughout the course. I was aware, as so often during my time in the Army, that the Church was being given a quite unique opportunity in courses such as these. Where else were men and women given such a chance in the course of their normal working life at the expense of their employers to explore the nature and relevance of the Christian faith? Attempts are not lacking to remove such remnants of Christian education as still remain in our state schools and no doubt similar efforts will be made to dislodge the Army and Services generally from their long-standing identification with the Christian faith. They will encounter stout resistance as far as the Army is concerned, and I have no doubt the Navy and the Air Force will be equally disinclined to agree that we should no longer strive to be a Christian country.

As the course took shape and the Centre got into its stride I began to feel that the peace-time Army was not for me. The SAS in war-time had been very different. The discipline we gladly accepted arose from the nature of the work in which we were engaged and was reinforced by complete confidence in the man at the top. Otherwise we enjoyed the maximum of freedom to carry out our particular task as we thought best. I concluded that, for better or worse, I was too much of an individualist to fit an increasingly rigid peace-time structure. I also felt the growing desire to settle somewhere where at least for a period I could put down some roots. The feeling was intensified by the arrival during our stay in Bagshot of our second son, Andrew. Army service would have meant splitting up the family in one way or another. For a combination of reasons I felt we ought to move, if we knew where. Once again the answer was provided for us, or so at least we believed.

I had been invited some months earlier to go to Dundee to address a group of local ministers, a Fraternal, on the subject of Christian education. The invitation came through the Reverend Ronald Thomson, minister of St. Stephens, Broughty Ferry, who had himself served throughout the war as a Chaplain with the 51st Highland Division. What I did not know at the time was that he was the Interim Moderator in the vacant charge of Broughty Ferry East. I don't recall mentioning to him that I thought of resigning my Army commission to return to civilian life, but some weeks later Ronald wrote to me suggesting that I might be 'heard' for the East Church. In the Church of Scotland ministers are called by the congregation which during any vacancy appoints a committee to 'hear' such ministers as may have applied for the church or may be thought possible by the committee. I accepted the suggestion and took services in St. Mary's, the Parish Church of Dundee. Before I left Dundee on the Sunday evening to return south Ronald telephoned the news that the Committee wished to recommend my appointment to the congregation. When in due course I appeared before the congregation, as regulations require, to conduct services as 'sole nominee', the congregation then proceeded to address to me the call to be their minister. Army days were ended and the work of a Scottish parish stretched ahead.

Chapter 8

Parish Minister in Broughty Ferry

Broughty Ferry lies snugly on the banks of the River Tay, familiar to many who might otherwise lack the knowledge of its existence through the rapture it inspired in the heart of Dundee's homespun poet, William McGonigal. Despite the ribbon development in between, the Ferry, as it is popularly known, is very much a community in its own right. I arrived ahead of the family and furniture in Earlville, the large and friendly house which was to be our home. It was far from empty. Soap and towels were waiting wherever they might be needed. The larder was stocked with provisions, mostly home-made. To crown all a cake model of Broughty Castle stood proudly on the kitchen table to thrill our two young sons when they arrived. This was the handiwork of one of our members, baker Alistair Goodfellow. What a heart-warming welcome it was to my first parish.

Some reassurance was needed. I was not at all disposed to underestimate my new responsibilities. I was well aware that the job of a parish minister was very different from any in which I had so far been engaged. I had never been asked to produce two sermons each week, or to preside over a Kirk Session and Deacons' Court – the two boards inherited from the United Free Church of Scotland responsible respectively for the spiritual care and business management of the congregation.

90

I had never been a member of a Presbytery, the court of the Church of Scotland to which congregations in its area are subject and to which they send their minister and representative elder to share in the conduct of its affairs. My confidence was not increased as I entered the vestry to find large, and, as it seemed to me, daunting photographs of my distinguished predecessors. Dr James Moffat, one of the great scholars of the Church and pioneer in Bible translation, had Principal James Denny, renowned theologian, as his companion. Looking at me with what I took to be a kindlier, if somewhat quizzical eye, was Dr Frank Cairns, now retired but still very much alive, and resident in Dundee.

He and I soon became fast friends. Although now a very old man, he was still well enough to preach on special occasions with much of his old fire and eloquence. He had entered the ministry later in life, after a career in business, and perhaps for that reason had never been able or willing to exchange his natural and at times aggressive forthrightness for the appropriate ecclesiastical bedside manner. As might have been expected, he succeeded in ruffling not a few of his affluent parishioners who may have wondered if this militant cleric quite knew his place. In complete, and no doubt very necessary, contrast, Mrs Cairns was the gentlest of women. She spent her years in the Ferry pouring soothing oil on the waters her unrepentant husband so consistently contrived to trouble. This process had continued so long that by the time we made their acquaintance Mrs Cairns had come to produce an involuntary Pavlov dog reaction whenever her husband opened his mouth. 'Oh Frank, oh Frank!' she would murmur deprecatingly, no matter how innocent his observation had been.

I knew the stories of the typical Scottish beadle, the officer charged with the care of the church, who carries the Bible to and from the pulpit at each service. I was fortunate to inherit Mr Joss, a former policeman and now a gardener. He was a man of very few words and grave demeanour, though not without a twinkle in his eye. He moved slowly and addressed himself to his tasks with great deliberation. He felt it his duty to keep the congregation and, no doubt, the new minister under close surveillance as the services proceeded. The consequences were sometimes surprising. The Communion Table stood directly under the pulpit and the plug which supplied power to the hearing aid system was under the Communion Table. A dear old lady, Mrs Keiller by name, sat near the front and invariably followed proceedings, by courtesy of her hearing aid, with the closest attention. On this occasion something had obviously gone wrong with the works. She shook the offending instrument, knocked it on the pew, twisted and turned it, but all to no avail. Then oblivious to my increasing embarrassment as I declaimed from the pulpit, she somehow succeeded in attracting the attention of our Mr Joss. He had clearly decided his course of action and moved majestically through the building to the chancel. Thereupon he disappeared from sight except for a pair of outsize legs which protruded interestingly from under the Communion Table. The plug was adjusted. Mrs Keiller gave a satisfied wave of her aid and Mr Joss went into reverse gear. The congregation removed its fascinated gaze and, I hope, tuned in to me again.

Any one of the legendary sayings of the beadles of the Kirk might have fallen from Mr Joss's judicious lips. I was never so incautious as to ask his opinion of a sermon, remembering the shattering come-back such a question had once produced for some unfortunate minister unnamed. 'You read your sermon,' said the beadle disapprovingly. 'You read it badly. Furthermore, it wasn't worth reading.'

Dr Malcolm Chalmers, to my mind the model general practitioner, was a member of the congregation. He became our family doctor and in addition our guide, philosopher and friend. No doubt he sensed the fact that I felt myself very much a new boy. He gave me his own recipe for success in the Ferry. 'Put a rose in your buttonhole,' he said, 'and hold your head high as you walk through the village.' Like any small and ingrown community it was inclined to be gossipy. The answer, in the view of one who knew the neighbourhood better than most, was to present a bold, if not brazen, front in all circumstances, at all times.

Broughty is a delightful place in which to live. From my study window, if my eyes ever strayed from my books, I looked out on the river and the green fields of the Kingdom of Fife. Most of the inhabitants were comfortably off. In earlier days some of the citizens, notably the jute barons, had been extremely wealthy. They vied with each other in building enormous residences, the most colossal of which, Castle Roy, was now empty and somewhat dilapidated and in use as an emergency centre for the homeless. Jute was still flourishing in the early fifties although, with increasing competition in India and elsewhere and advances in technology, the writing was already on the wall. The congregation, numbering around five hundred, was predominantly middle class, but represented a fair cross-section of the population. At one end of the financial scale was our meticulous church treasurer, William Smail, managing director of Low and Bonar, jute spinners and engineers. He and his wife were the kindest of friends – our relationship even surviving the strain of journeys in his outsize motor-car, in which he refused to be driven at speeds exceeding thirty miles an hour, irrespective of the distance involved. At the other end was Grannie Henderson, whose husband, a former seaman, had delivered coal locally until failing sight compelled him to retire. I had no firmer allies than the Hendersons, and no more outspoken critic than Grannie. She felt entirely uninhibited in her comments on my preaching. I remember being in their little cottage near the shore one Monday morning to enquire for Mr Henderson who by this time was critically ill. 'You were very good yesterday,' said Grannie. 'I'll no say you are always good.' I could see that my aim must be to be as good as possible as often as possible. As far as Scotland is concerned the sermon is the magnet. Numbers attending depend on the interest and helpfulness of the preaching.

How easy it is to give the claims of preaching less than the priority they deserve. There are so many things needed to be done. When the weekend is over the next Sunday seems a long and a safe distance away. Meantime there are marriages and funerals, committees and organisations, and a never-ending list of visits to be paid; not to mention local community activities calling for Christian concern and support. Certainly it would be wrong to withdraw regularly and stubbornly from so many worthwhile activities unless, by failing to do so, we should be breaking faith with our own ordination as we most certainly would. We are ordained to the ministry of Word and Sacrament. How shall we ensure that we declare the Word of God unless we are ourselves continually listeners? In study and in prayer we are to receive that Word made flesh in Jesus Christ and share Him with our people. We have no greater gift to offer. There is none.

None with greater relevance for individual and social need. Here in Holy Scripture is the Royal Law, for everyone everywhere in every age. Here is the will of God for men and for nations. It is a social and political gospel just as much as it is individual and personal. Detailed party political programmes will not be found in the Bible, nor should they be voiced from the pulpit. What will most certainly be found are those inalienable principles governing human behaviour which governments of any colour, like individual men and women, disregard at their peril, and which demand to be reflected in codes of conduct whether individual or social, national or international. The Bible demolishes the wall we constantly seek to build dividing the sacred from the secular. The Bible demands that we live in one world which is God's world in God's way. The world will not know this unless it is told and we, the Ministers of the Word, are there to tell it. No amount of busy-ness, however estimable, can excuse neglect of this priority and privilege.

The news is frequently unwelcome, and so the preacher is frequently at risk; never more so than in our own day, as Dietrich Bonhoeffer, Archbishop Romero, Father Popieluszko and Archbishop Tutu bear witness. It is quite true that they can be called political meddlers as their persecutors allege, but not in any narrow, party sense; only to the extent that God is Himself a meddler, an intruder on the social and political scene, making His own demands and declaring His sovereign will in Jesus Christ, His Son.

We ought indeed to thank God that our position in this country is vastly different from that obtaining in South America, in Russia, in South Africa, or in any of the areas in which those in power are consistently committed to policies patently un-Christian. Thankfulness however is no justification for complacency. Our nation could not be in more urgent need of Christian Evangelism. The Christian capital, which we have to thank for so much that is worthy in our nation's life, is rapidly being expended and not being replaced. We drift further and further away from goodness. Since goodness is the by-product of right conviction this is hardly surprising. Statistics have been called the ultimate in lies but they certainly tell the truth when they reveal the moral landslide which has defaced our country in the last fifty years. Figures for marriage break-down reveal the growing instability of our national home life. Child abuse makes it urgently necessary to protect children from their own parents. It is increasingly perilous to be a policeman, or a teacher, or a social worker. Hostels for battered wives are required. Young and old alike fear for their safety as they walk our streets and travel on our trains. It has become necessary to post notices in shops to the effect that stealing will not be tolerated, since so many take it for granted. The services of our hard pressed police have to be supplemented by private security firms. Dishonesty has raised its ugly head in what used to be regarded as the citadel of probity in the City of London. The so-called Good Old Days were certainly not all they are sometimes cracked up to be for everyone but they were characterised by a widely held view of what was right and what was wrong, a view born and nurtured in Christian faith. Our present moral plight will find no healing without a rebirth of that faith. For its own sake and that of the wider world, our country must be won for faith in Jesus Christ. How will it hear of Him and the life to which He calls without a preacher? It is not given to many to declare the message with the eloquence of a Charles H. Spurgeon or a James S. Stewart. It may well be true that the days of great preaching are past. It is not true that the message is any less great or less powerful when proclaimed with sincerity and humility. That message condemns whatever is base in the life of men and nations and summons us to work and pray, to live and be prepared to die for the true welfare of our fellow men, in this country and throughout the world, whatever their colour or creed may be.

If the minister is to be found faithful here his or her time and energies must be directed to that end. Initial theological training is essential, but if we cease to be students when the College course is over our ministry and the congregations we serve will be progressively impoverished. The Bible must be our daily companion and our daily teacher, as must the aids to Bible study which now abound in commentaries and imaginative modern translations. We need to acquaint ourselves with the work of gifted expositors of an earlier day and our own. We must have some knowledge of the working assumptions of our contemporaries in literature, in the arts, in politics, in industry, in the commercial world, in science. We must make time for the 'heavies' of the newspaper world and one or other of the journals which make a serious attempt to read the signs of the times. It is normally possible to keep mornings clear for the tasks of study. This is top priority. Some time, too, must be found for those radio and television programmes which are so increasingly influential for good or ill. If all this sounds like counsels of perfection I readily acknowledge that my own record in these respects is a very imperfect one. Nevertheless I did my best to establish such a study routine and have been thankful for it ever since. It demands a good deal in the way of self discipline. Other members of the community have to report for work at a given time. The minister has to be his own boss and form the habit of regular and early rising if the morning is not to disappear. I appreciate that until stipends are fair and adequate the minister's wife may have to be an earner too, if she can. In this case housekeeping chores make serious inroads on the minister's time for study and preparation. The Church of Scotland may be a better employer than some other denominations, but all alike fail to make adequate provision for their full-time employees.

If a minister must study regularly, it is no less essential that he pray. Manuals of inspiration abound as do collections of prayers for daily use. These have helped me enormously and continue to do so. *A Chain of Prayer across the Ages* was recommended to us in student days by Professor H.R. Mackintosh who confessed that he used it himself every day. If such a saint and scholar needed such assistance there was no doubt we would need it too.

The late James Kyd Thomson, the minister to whom I can never overstate my debt, made this entry in his diary. 'Resolved to double the time I spend in prayer each day and to preach on the results.' There cannot fail to be results, in the life of the one who prays and in the lives of those for whom we pray. I have suggested how, as I believe, the hand of God may be discerned in my own life. I have no doubt that had I been more faithful in daily prayer the evidence would be infinitely more striking. Even as it is I find there is proof enough, accumulating daily as in situations and opportunities of one kind and another I find reason to believe that I have been sent where God wanted me to be and enabled in some measure to be a strength and comfort to my fellow men. 'When I pray,' wrote William Temple, 'I find "coincidences" happen.' The Christian life is a guided life and the key to that guidance is daily humble and believing prayer, speaking to God as a child might speak to a wise and loving father.

We may and should speak for others as well as for ourselves. Indeed for many of us it is likely to be concern for someone else which prompts prayer. Ministers have no monopoly of intercession but ministers have a binding obligation to pray for as well as with their people. 'Far be it from me,' said Samuel (I Samuel 12:23), 'that I should sin against the Lord by ceasing to pray for you.' That text might well be framed and hung in every study. The vocation of monk or nun is not for every Christian but no Christian should doubt its value. 'More things are wrought by prayer than this world dreams of.' Working for what is God's will may indeed be a kind of praying, but for the work of prayer itself there is no substitute. For most of us the legitimate demands of daily work leave but little time for conscious communion with God. How thankful we should be for those who feel led to contract out of the obligations most of us accept if the work of the world is to go on. By their ceaseless ministry of prayer that work is underpinned and transformed.

I am so sure of this that if I were to begin my ministry again with the insights I now possess I would spend far more time each day in prayer for particular people as their special needs were known to me. Of course intercession is a mystery, like most of the greatest things in life. Why should music move us as

it does, or some painting, or some book? Why should love
wake us, as the poet claims, from the slumber of insensitivity?
We can only answer, in the ultimate, that this does happen.
God has so ordained that we may help our fellow-men as we
bring them to Him in prayer for His blessing. Only in heaven
can we expect to understand more fully why this should be so
but here and now we can know enough to lead us to pray for
others with confidence. A critic of Turner turned away con-
temptuously from one of his pictures exclaiming, 'I never saw a
sunset like that.' Turner was standing nearby and answered,
'Don't you wish you had?' Life is transformed as we discover
the power of prayer for others as for ourselves and the discovery
is open to us all.

If the mornings are well spent the afternoons and evenings are
more likely to look after themselves. In the normal parish a
large part of the minister's time should be claimed by the
visitation of those who are ill or in some special need and the
visitation of members in their own homes. The necessity of the
former is clear enough and in my view there is no substitute for
the latter. Congregations ought to be small enough or church
staffs large enough to make it possible. When the minister visits
in the home he makes it clear that he cares about his people and
wants to know them better. In most cases at least he becomes
the trusted friend of the family, whether or not it should be
'kirk greedy'. Before the visit ends there should be opportunity
for a brief act of family worship in which the Bible is read and
prayer is offered. In many cases, perhaps most, the practice of
family prayers has long since disappeared. It is hardly likely to
be re-established if the minister fails to give such a lead.

A Church of Scotland congregation is divided into districts,
each one of which is under the care of an elder. On my first
round of congregational visitation the elder of the particular
district accompanied me, which was a help to us both. Elders
have the responsibility of visiting each home on their list and

sharing with the minister in the pastoral care of the flock. To some this presents no problem but others may feel ill at ease on their calls. The minister who has been specially trained for the work can inspire confidence in cases where it is very much needed. On the other hand, the elder can often effect introductions and keep the minister's feet firmly on the ground of the local situation. In the East Church I had the companionship of a number of devoted and experienced elders led by the Clerk to the Kirk Session, Bob Nicol, a retired headmaster and as ideal a right hand man as any minister could wish to have. How much I owe to his judgement and encouragement and affection for me and mine.

Archbishop Temple has said that what he covets most of all in the Church of Scotland is the institution of the eldership. The elder is a layman who is 'ordained' to the rule and pastoral care of the congregation. The ruling part of his duties consists in sharing in the deliberations of the Kirk Session, charged with the administration of the congregation in the context of the Church of Scotland law. The minister is Moderator or Chairman of the Session. As far as pastoral care is concerned the elder is no longer expected to catechise the members of his district as once was the case. He is enjoined to take time and trouble to know them and to make a real effort to share his own faith with them. In recent years increasing attention has been paid in Scotland to the elder's role. In many areas training courses are available and efforts made to realise the full potential of the office. For some years now the eldership has been open to women, as is now the ministry also. In both spheres women give distinguished and much needed service – an undoubted fact of which it is to be hoped our sister communions will take note.

The minister of the Church of Scotland is also minister of the parish whose bounds are determined by the Presbytery. My parish included the local Education Authority non-feepaying school, the Eastern by name. Scots are wont to boast of their educational system and the Eastern provided good reason. It was, and is, a Primary School taking pupils from entry at the age of five to the point of their 'Eleven Plus' examination as it was then called. Kenneth and Andrew were both pupils there. The Infant Department, a model of its kind, was under the direction of one of our office-bearers, Miss Alison Crystal. The headmaster, Willie Wilson, a footballer of repute and a born teacher, combined kindliness and efficiency.

As parish minister I was expected to visit the classes in turn and thus supplement the religious instruction given by the teacher. The time involved each week was not considerable but it was long enough to give me some insight into the teacher's task. I have never subsequently been in any doubt that the teaching profession is one of the most demanding. To win and keep the interest of your class is no mean feat, even for a short period. To do so day in and day out throughout the year is to my mind one of the hardest jobs in the world. Some forty years later, in those areas where discipline has vanished, it has become wholly impossible.

At Christmas and Easter, and on other special occasions, the entire school crossed the road and came to church. This was a new and at first an alarming experience for me. I had realised that they would be prepared to listen to some sort of story. If it had any merit at all you could have heard a pin drop. If, however, I passed on from the story to point some kind of moral the entire assembly cleared its throat, changed position, shuffled its eight or nine hundred feet and indicated quite unmistakably that the show was over and they had switched off. I learned that the moral had to be inside the story or nowhere at all. Provided I bore this elementary point in mind boys and girls ranging from five to eleven or twelve in age would listen in rapt attention and the minister would enjoy the occasion as much as they did. I learned, too, what pleasure they had in singing, so long as they knew and approved of the hymns, and how infinitely seriously they took any part in the service allotted to them. Somewhere in the School may still be found the cup, not a valuable one but all I could afford, which I gave for presentation to any boy or girl judged to have made a particularly valuable contribution to the School. It was a very inadequate expression of appreciation of what it had done, both for the boys and for me.

I suppose we are all tempted to idealise the past but I cannot imagine that the five years we spent in the Ferry could have been happier or more filled with interest and encouragement. The congregation grew in numbers and activity. Accommodation was found nearby for a Sunday morning creche – a new venture in those days. Congregational reactions to such innovations as Christmas Eve Candlelight services and Easter Flower services were cautious at first but never obstructive, and, as time passed, enthusiastic. Religious broadcasting, in which I was allowed to play a regular part, gave us the opportunity of doing a month's 'People's Service' which resulted in a large and demanding postbag. The *Evening Telegraph*, which had serialised my book *Parachute Padre*, invited me to contribute a weekly column to their Saturday church page. This column, which I was to write for some ten years, strengthened our contacts with the community and taught me many a valued lesson in the art of popular communication. I could have had no kinder or more expert teacher than the then editor of the *Telegraph*, the late Ralph Pride. For the first time I learned what 'hard news' meant and finally and forever got it fixed in my head that to be sold in any particular literary market contributions had to be tailor-made to that end. It was also impressed upon me in the nicest and firmest way that even when McLuskey had written something down with considerable care it could, and frequently should, be radically altered – or even omitted altogether! 'Grannie' Henderson's robust reactions to my performance in the pulpit were paralleled by Pride's more sophisticated criticisms of my journalistic efforts. However, I continued to be published and paid rather than damned, so concluded that I must be more or less on the right lines.

With the care of a young family and a large and demanding manse, Irene was not expected to assume the leadership of the Woman's Guild which in those days so often devolved on the minister's wife. She did play an active part in its life and enjoyed the happiest of relations with the congregation. Friendships were made which have continued through the years. How rich the ministry can be in personal relationships and how infinitely rewarding. Proof of friendship was provided in the most practical way. A car was beyond our means but whenever one was required for the job I had only to ask one of several generous and trusting car owners. I have particularly pleasant and grateful memories of baker Willie Goodfellow's Alvis – a joy for any keen driver to handle. It carried me around the country at speed when I was doing some discussion broadcasts with Ronnie Falconer, the then head of religious broadcasting in Scotland. I did eventually acquire a motor cycle and then, after my father's death, the little Austin van he had obtained for his agency work. When we moved back to Scotland he was still at work in Kirkcaldy making at least enough to cover his lodgings there and weekend journeys to Edinburgh. We were glad to be nearer him and he enjoyed greatly the opportunity of getting to know the boys, who were devoted to him. He knew instinctively what would give them pleasure and I know their response to his fun and his visits to the Ferry brought some comfort and happiness to the last years of his life. The series of tough breaks had not succeeded in embittering him or robbing him of his ability to see the amusing side of things. I had never known him other than kind and gentle, and enduringly and humblingly proud of his children.

The care of a small and compact congregation still left time and energy for additional responsibilities. The Church of

Scotland works through a number of committees charged with the oversight of Church of Scotland concerns at home and overseas. I served for a period on those dealing with Youth and what were then called Colonial and Continental Missions before joining one in which I was specially interested, the Inter-Church Relations Committee. For some time I had been involved with the British Council of Churches and had attended the first meeting of the World Council of Churches in Amsterdam in 1948. I had the equal good fortune to attend the second in Evanston in 1954. My early training in the SCM had introduced me to the ecumenical world and convinced me, in the words of one of its pioneers, that the world is too strong for a divided Church. It was and is the task of Inter-Church Relations to interpret the insights and demands of the ecumenical movement to the Church of Scotland and to explore the possibilities of growth toward a fuller unity for the various denominations in Scotland. Spectacular results have so far eluded us but the search continues. I cannot conceive it will ever be abandoned until the Church of Jesus Christ in Scotland is known and seen to be one.

My term in Broughty Ferry coincided with the launching of the Billy Graham Crusades in London and Glasgow. I had the opportunity of hearing Dr Graham preach in Harringey and subsequently came to know him, and his wife Ruth, as valued friends. Although her husband is a Baptist Ruth is a Presbyterian; at a later stage, when the Graham Mission returned to London, Ruth worshipped with us regularly in St. Columba's of which I was then the minister.

Like many other congregations, we in the East Church arranged a coach to take interested members to the Glasgow Crusade. One of my elders, John Sherard, felt led as a result to offer for the ministry. To give up his secure job and to put the care of his wife and two children at risk was not easy, but it was done. In due course he qualified and was called to a parish. Some fifteen years later he and his wife Mary saw their son Dane complete his course of training for the ministry. How vast is the number of ministers of different denominations whom we owe under God to the Graham Crusades.

I thank God for them. They have been criticised for 'pressurising'. The massed choirs, the highly skilled Master of Ceremonies, Cliff Barrows, the brilliant pianist, the throbbing bass tones of Beverly Shea as he sings the simple and memorable melodies, the hypnotic power of Billy Graham himself as he calls people forward to give themselves to Christ – all this, we are sometimes told, is designed to produce a mass-generated emotional impulse rather than a responsible decision to follow Jesus. I think the real cause for concern is not what happens on the night of the Crusade but what happens, or fails to happen, thereafter. Every effort is made to link those who come forward with the Church in their own area. Where the man or woman concerned is welcomed with warmth and sympathy in the local congregation their decision 'on the night' may, and not infrequently does, result in a continuing life of Christian faith and worship and service. The fact that so much depends on the follow-up must not be allowed to detract from the value and importance of the spiritual experience which, praise God, has come and keeps coming to countless men and women during the Graham Crusades.

Parish duties had a delightful and instructive interlude when I was given the opportunity by the British Council of Churches to visit the United States.

The Inter-Church Preachers Scheme was designed to exchange a group of ministers of different denominations from Britain with a similar number from the United States. It was operated by the British Council of Churches and the National Council of Churches in the United States. As the English

Speaking Union in America collaborated and secured offers of hospitality the minister from this country could usually finance the trip at small or no cost to himself. The preaching fees in the States are much larger than those provided here so the American visitors are less fortunate, but as a rule they are in a better position to make up any deficit incurred.

I was to visit America on subsequent occasions but no later stay in the country could compare in excitement with the first. I travelled over tourist class on the latest American acquisition to their Atlantic fleet, the *United States*. How glad I was to make the first visit by sea. To sail up the Hudson River as the Statue of Liberty and the Manhattan skyline came into view was an unforgettable experience. Equally memorable was an incident as I waited to get to the gangway. An American citizen was at my side, talking in a typically free and friendly way. He asked me what took me to New York and where I was going to stay. I said I would be accommodated in a flat kindly offered to visiting preachers by Lewis Douglas, recently United States Ambassador to Britain.

'You're with a politician,' he exclaimed. 'You'll be through the customs in record time.' The implication was clear. Politicians were apparently thought to enjoy special privileges which their friends might expect to share. I had reason to recall the observation as my stay in America lengthened. The impression grew that while political life in this country is certainly not entirely free from corruption the extent prevailing in the States is very much greater. It is more difficult to imagine a Watergate here.

I visited the States in the fifties when the post-war religious boom there was at its height. It was mainly a middle and upper class phenomenon but on these levels of society the Church was a force to be reckoned with. Church-going was the rule rather than the exception and support for the work of the Church at home and abroad was of a generous order, far exceeding anything one knew in Britain. Church 'plant' in the case of the larger congregations by our standards was on a lavish scale. Church staffs provided for secretarial and administrative officials, while ministerial appointments allowed for specialisation in education and pastoral care and counselling. Smaller and less affluent congregations had to be content with premises and staff more akin to the British pattern. The boom times have passed and financial recession has left its mark in America as elsewhere, but it is still true that American churches appreciate the need to be as well equipped for their tasks as any business organisation. They are equally aware that if this is to be possible Christian stewardship has to be taken seriously by church members. A 'small change' attitude to Christian giving has long since been challenged and exposed. The forthright common sense which is so typical of the average American is not left behind when he enters the church door as is unfortunately so often the case in this country.

The Christian Church in a secular state has a big job on its hands. State education in America makes no provision for religious instruction with the result that the churches must conduct and finance their own Christian education programmes. Until recently the position was very different here, but it is changing rapidly. As our nation becomes more and more racially mixed and religiously pluralistic and as the Christian Church grows less influential the situation may become very similar to that in the States. There will then be the same challenge to the churches to provide instruction no longer available in most schools and in most homes. If this is to be done, finance and trained personnel will be required on a scale far beyond present resources. By the same token church members in this country will need to scale up their contributions in as realistic and generous a fashion as their American counterparts.

The ten weeks I spent in the States could only have been more enjoyable if finances had permitted Irene and the boys to be with me. The churches I visited were of very different kinds, but all equally welcoming. In New York itself I was invited to preach in St. Bartholomew's Protestant Episcopal Church, a truly magnificent basilican structure with music and appointments to match. I was doubly fortunate since the invitation carried with it another, to spend a week with Mr and Mrs Stewart Duncan in their residence at Newport, Rhode Island. Knowing nothing of what such an invitation might import, I packed the minimum of belongings in my battered hold-all and took the train recommended. At the station I was met by a liveried chauffeur in charge of two gigantic vehicles. One, a limousine, was for me. The other, a shooting brake, was for my non-existent luggage. On the way to the Tudor style mansion, brought over brick by brick from England, the chauffeur gently prepared me for the scale of affluence I was soon to encounter. The butler who awaited me in the hall continued the process. When my miserably inadequate wardrobe was laid out by some lesser member of staff he reappeared and did his best to reassure me. They dressed for dinner, he said. I had to confess that such evening clothes as I possessed were on the wrong side of the Atlantic. The situation, however, was not irretrievable. I had by some stroke of good fortune a dark suit and the butler promised me a dark bow tie which gave me each evening at least a veneer of respectability.

Life with the Duncans was on a level of magnificence of which I had only read. There were cars in the garage, all of mammoth proportions, for every day of the week and no doubt two for Sundays. For bathing they had access to the adjacent and highly exclusive Bailley's Beach, where I was ready to believe the waters of the Atlantic had first been specially processed. Dinner parties were on a scale to match. It might all have proved too much for a young Scots minister, by comparison so under-privileged, had it not been for the Duncans themselves. Mrs Duncan's father had been a Presbyterian minister and she treasured her recollections of the manse of her youth. As far as she was concerned I could more than repay their fabulous hospitality by playing Scottish airs on their grand piano. Mr Duncan had put Lea and Perrins sauce on the map and himself in the millionaire category but his kindness of heart had not been jettisoned on the way to the top. No host or hostess could have been more gracious or done more to make my days in Newport as happy as they proved to be.

Not every weekend was on such a level. In Summit, New Jersey I spent ten days at a hotel as guest of the local Baptist Church. My itinerary took me more briefly to Providence, Rhode Island, and Hartford and Bridgeport, Connecticut. There were speaking engagements in the University of Ann Arbor, Michigan, and at a summer youth camp on the shores of the lovely Lake Winnepesauki, New Hampshire. Most memorable of all were the days I spent as guest preacher at the Presbyterian Conference Centre in Massanetta Springs in the Blue Ridge Mountains of Virginia.

The conference centre there is still going strong. Just as Keswick in the English Lake District is the gathering point for the spiritual recharging of British evangelicals, so Massanetta is the Mecca of America ministers and their wives and members in search of fellowship and inspiration. Speakers from the States and further afield are assembled to offer their interpretations of the Christian faith. I imagine that today the voice of the radical is heard more often than in the less troubled days of the early fifties. The cosiness I remember so well could hardly be expected to survive the McCarthy era of reds under the beds, much less the volcanic spasms of Vietnam.

The idyllic setting of Massanetta combined with the glorious summer weather and the warmth of the friendship everywhere extended contributed to my deep and lasting appreciation of my stay in the States. I didn't need the complete surprise of my homeward journey to convince me that America was a wonderful country but I had it just the same. I was booked to return on the same splendid *United States* and once again with the cheapest ticket obtainable. On reaching the point of embarkation I lost touch with my luggage. On enquiry, I found that both the luggage and I had been switched to the first class section. 'Mr Mitchell has arranged this,' they said. I then recalled that Mr Mitchell had stayed at the Summit Hotel where I had been a guest. We had talked occasionally and he had enquired for the reason of my visit. I learned he was connected with the United States Line and so I mentioned my pleasure in travelling on the *United States*. I remembered now that he said casually that they would take good care of me on my way home. He had now proved as good as his word. As President of the line, as I was subsequently to learn, his word could hardly be gainsaid. I wondered if there would be time to telephone my thanks to Mr Mitchell before the ship left. I need not have worried. There in the cabin was the great man himself, checking, no doubt, on his fairy godfather instructions. He cut short my thanks. 'You can do something for us,' he said. 'You can take the service on Sunday.' I was in a mood to take as many services as he might care any and every day of the week.

I realised very well that my visit could hardly yield more than a superficial grasp of life in such an enormous melting-pot of so many races and so many cultures. My travels had been mainly confined to the New England states. As far as Church life was concerned, I had only been introduced to a tiny section of the more affluent congregations. I was to learn later from Bruce Kenrick's *Come out the Wilderness* of the exciting and heroic Christian witness in East Harlem. I knew nothing of the Church of the Saviour in Washington when I paid a brief visit there. The story of that congregation's endeavour to be a costly and caring community has been an inspiration to me as to so many others through the years. Preparation for full membership is long and demanding. Giving in terms of money and community service is on a scale to which few Christian groups in any country could begin to approximate. Church membership in the States still remains predominantly middle and upper class as we would reckon these categories but it has become more difficult for the critics today to write off Church allegiance in terms of social convention. In churches of all denominations there has been an abundant supply of men and women willing to stand up and be counted in the struggle for racial justice and equality. When the story of America in the second half of this century is written it will be recorded, electronic evangelism notwithstanding, that the American Churches have been in the van of the struggle for human rights both abroad and at home.

Chapter 9

Parish Minister in Bearsden, Glasgow

Our departure from Broughty Ferry was as unexpected as our move north five years before. Dr Nevile Davidson, then minister of Glasgow Cathedral, had invited me as one of their summer preachers. On the Sunday of my visit some members of the vacancy committee from New Kilpatrick Parish Church, Bearsden, on the outskirts of Glasgow, attended the service to 'hear' me, as the expression goes. In due course I was invited to be their minister. In November 1955 we moved to our new home in Bearsden. Irene and I were as sorry to be leaving Broughty Ferry as I was thrilled to be tackling my new job. The congregation of New Kilpatrick, one of the largest in Scotland, was over two thousand strong – four times larger than my previous flock. It was the original parish church of Bearsden and the surrounding countryside, with a history stretching back over three hundred years. With the birth of each daughter church, required as population expanded, its parish had been reduced, but it was still a large one, including the original village of Bearsden and embracing farms, of which the whole district had once been mainly composed. Our glebe, a large field adjacent to the manse, normally had one of the farm horses as its occupant, to the great delight of our young sons, and indeed my own. Bearsden still retained the character of a village community but was growing by leaps and bounds as it became an increasingly coveted section of the Glasgow commuter belt. Young couples poured in as soon as there were houses ready for them or their firms to buy. In many cases they already had church connections or were very ready to make them. It would have been surprising if the congregation had not grown steadily or failed to be representative of the business and professional life of Scotland's largest city. No situation could possibly have provided greater stimulus or encouragement to a parish minister.

After the long and faithful ministry of my predecessor, Dr James McCardel, the congregation was in very good heart and ready for any expansion of its activities. The Sunday School was large and soon became enormous. From the age group fourteen to seventeen, renowned even then for its problems, there was a ready response to Junior and Senior Bible Classes, which together soon numbered a hundred or more. Capable leaders were found for a Sunday morning creche. A large and active Young Wives Group sprang up as the companion to a no less vigorous Woman's Guild. Easter Flower and Christmas Eve Candlelight services were welcomed with enthusiasm. Irene and I had particular pleasure in the Saturday evening Socials we arranged for each district in turn until the whole congregation had been covered. The friendliness and warmth of the people in the West of Scotland is well known but we found that there was still need for members of the congregation to get to know one another better. The Socials made an important contribution to this end.

'Knocking' the Church is an activity popular with some outside, and indeed not a few inside, its ranks. It is pleasant to record that New Kilpatrick in the years that I knew it was as happy a congregation as it was vigorous. We had joy in our worship together and in the activities of the different age groups which it was our honest intention should be the strengthening of the cause of Jesus Christ among our fellowmen. Ministers, like those of any other calling, can have formidable difficulties with their people. Church officials can impede rather than co-operate. Members of the congregation can take umbrage with or without reason. Choirs can be awkward, determined to sit in the wrong places and sing at the wrong time in the wrong way. Organists can be in business for themselves. Leaders of organisations can quarrel over limited accommodation. Any change can meet with determined and unreasoning opposition. Dr George Cameron, later to be my colleague in London, tells the story of the Beadle who gave this advice to his successor: 'Above all else, resist any innovation.' Such an attitude not infrequently characterises the congregations ministers are appointed to serve. The position of New Kilpatrick could not have been more different. The Clerk to the Kirk Session, James Gordon, was as efficient as he was kindly. Our energetic Finance Convener was Berend Shaw, well known in Glasgow shipping circles and a pillar of the Boys' Brigade. He rejoiced in the loudest laugh I can recall. A retired banker, Hugh Millar, kept the roll of members with meticulous care. Our senior elder, William Aitken, for long factor to the Garscube estates, looked after the church property with loving and unfailing care. In Kenneth MacLellan, a most active elder, we possessed one of Scotland's leading evangelicals who never failed to combine zeal for his Master with loving kindness toward his fellow-men. One of my most interesting and rewarding assignments was to conduct worship in the MacLellan factory in Maryhill where work stopped during the busy, noisy day for the purpose. Harry MacGill, music master in the High School of Glasgow, was our organist and, like the members of his choir, an unfailingly sympathetic member of the church team. Last, but by no means least, our Church Officer was Thomas Kilgour, a painter by trade, and the most gracious of men. My robes still hang on the 'shoulders' on which he lettered my initials. With all my colleagues, as with so many other members of the congregation, Irene and I formed lasting friendships.

In many cases my duties were a continuation of those to which I had grown accustomed in Broughty Ferry but there were new and interesting responsibilities too. Westerton, Scotland's first garden suburb, was part of our parish but had now grown to the point of requiring its own church. The necessary arrangements with the ecclesiastical and civil authorities were eventually completed and a new building dedicated and a new congregation launched. New Kilpatrick itself was greatly in need of a chapel within the church itself. Thanks to the generous gift of Miss Winifred Paterson, one of our oldest members, and the services, no less generous, of William Smith, then Professor of Architecture in Glasgow's Technical College, a very lovely chapel was created. The pastoral care of the congregation was enormously strengthened by the appointment of Mrs Ian Gordon as Church Secretary.

It is not unknown for neighbouring congregations to display a certain rivalry, friendly or unfriendly. In Bearsden the three congregations of the Church of Scotland enjoyed the closest and happiest of relationships. All three ministers, under the leadership of Dr George MacLennan, the father of the community by reason of seniority and quite outstanding gifts, planned their work together and worked as a united team. There was a small but active congregation of the Scottish Episcopal Church with which we had an invariably helpful association. Under the auspices of the Tell Scotland campaign a parish mission and house to house visitation was undertaken by church members on a completely interdenominational basis. To a degree I have never known elsewhere church and community were one.

The only serious problems we encountered in our first four years in Bearsden were concerned with the manse. Long before our arrival it had been afflicted with extensive dry rot. Soon thereafter it fell victim to this dread disease once again. In a matter of months whole areas of the house became uninhabitable. Our plight was not improved when so-called experts arrived to burn out the affected areas and set the whole wing ablaze. Before long one kitchen wall was missing, while we literally walked the plank to pass from the front door to such rooms on the ground floor as could still be used. We were finally driven to seek refuge in a hotel, but by that time a blow had fallen which made the ravages of dry rot appear of small consequence.

Irene had seemed her usual energetic and healthy self. Even when the swelling appeared on one breast we were not immediately anxious. Analysis was to provide ample cause for concern. Surgical treatment was carried out but the disease followed its all too usual and tragic course. We both knew how it was almost certain to end. After nine months of increasing weakness and discomfort which she bore with uncomplaining courage, Irene died.

Kenneth was then fourteen and Andrew twelve and they were as devoted to their mother as any boys could be. Both took the loss more bravely and unselfishly than I could have anticipated. I had no idea at all how hardly I would take the experience of bereavement and had gravely over-estimated my ability to cope with the situation. I knew what seemed certain to happen and had been glad to think that I would be left on my own rather than Irene. How wrong I was! Apart from the problem of financing the home I have no doubt that Irene would have found it easier to go on without me than I did without her. This seemed all the stranger since in a sense bereavements were part of my business. I knew what it was to feel with others in their grief, to pray with and for them, to try in every way I could to comfort them. I was surprised to find how little my professional experience had prepared me for the blow which had now fallen. I could not have felt more broken or bereft. Left to myself I could not have faced the future.

Fortunately for me I had sons to look after. For their sakes I had to keep going. Fortunately too I had work to do which refused to wait until I felt better. Perhaps it was foolish to fulfil my engagement to take televised evening prayers on the day of her death but I thought it was what Irene would wish me to do. The day to day responsibilities of my calling held me up, as did the love and the prayers of countless friends. Two in particular come to mind. They lived nearby and guessed that the ending of the day would be the worst time for me. Time and again they called in late in the evening and transformed the strangely empty manse with the boys in bed asleep and no Irene.

The assurance of life after death is an essential part of Christian faith, as certain as the Resurrection of our Lord and His promise that in our Father's house there are many mansions. Surely as a minister of the church and a convinced believer I had resources which ought to have transformed the experience of bereavement. To some real extent this was certainly the case. I did and do believe that the parting is not forever. I did and do look forward to reunion 'on the further shore'. But in the meantime life was suddenly and agonisingly empty where once it had been gloriously full. No reliance on a heaven almost wholly beyond our powers to conceive could at that time of loss bring much in the way of comfort. The inescapable duties of this world were much more help to me, as was my love for the boys and their love for me. I was desperately afraid to let them down. I had no sense of any loss of communion with God or any indignation that our prayers for Irene's recovery had not been granted. I knew enough of the world we live in to realise that others had daily much tougher breaks than mine. It was easier for me to go on praying as more than ever I realised my own weakness and insufficiency. I had learned a lesson which I don't think I have ever long forgotten. I was not the rocklike character I had fancied myself to be. I was not the partner better able to be on my own. I did not have the strength to pick myself up and carry on. I asked for the strength daily and have never had the least doubt where it came from. One well-wisher wrote in sympathy when Irene died. I have often recollected the letter as an example of what not to say. He referred to the hope that I would be upheld in the long, lonely years ahead. The one thing we should never be asked in such circumstances is to look any distance ahead, but simply to concentrate on one day and its demands at a time.

I don't think I have ever lacked real sympathy for those in bereavement but I know now that you have to pass through the dark valley yourself before you can understand at least in some measure what it means to someone else. I believe God has used my experience of loss to equip me to help others in their time of dire need. Indeed, in a manner I could certainly never have foreseen, the attempt to be of some use in another's tragic loss was one day to open a happier chapter for me.

I can also say from what I have learned myself that time can be the healer it is often claimed to be. The statement requires qualification. Time can also succeed in keeping the wound open if we are determined it shall never be closed. If, however, we make a real attempt to begin again; if we humbly and gratefully accept what good friends can offer; if we try to do anything in our power for others; if we resolutely struggle to keep looking outward rather than inward to our broken heart; if, above all, we take our weakness and misery and insufficiency to God in simple, childlike prayer, then indeed the passage of time can and does heal and renew us.

I can pinpoint the actual moment when this came home to me. Irene had been dead for some two years. The move to London had taken place and I was taking my Golden Labrador, Sam, for his daily walk in Hyde Park. Suddenly, and for no apparent reason, I knew that the Park looked very beautiful and that I was enjoying myself. I felt as if a very heavy load had just been lifted from my shoulders so that now my step could be lighter. I don't mean that loneliness and longing were there and then forever banished, but I realised in that instant that life might be happy again.

Chapter 10

Minister Minus a Parish in London

City of the dead:
Offices, shops, banks, warehouses,
Sullen, deserted.

Except where there is food, wine, music,
Restless rhythm:
And restless rhythmic searching of the young
In street and park for satisfaction
Of a restlessness within.

Dark London streets
Breathing a peace
That we have lost.

If you want to know the time, so the old song runs, ask a
policeman. If you should take that counsel in London it is more
than likely that a Scots voice will reply. Scottish immigrants
form a substantial part of the force as they do in so many areas
of the life of the capital. The Civil Service, accountancy, bank-
ing, law, nursing, engineering, medicine, all record similar
infiltration. It may be claimed also that in most cases the London Scot has got on very well. The story is told of an Edinburgh man who was posted for a short spell of duty in London.

On his return home he was asked how he had found the English. 'I didn't meet many,' he replied. 'You see, I was only dealing with heads of departments.' He found it unnecessary to add that these had all been Scots! In recent years as oil developments have provided a much needed fillip to the Scottish economy the drift south has been reduced but the number of London Scots is still considerable.

They need not be deprived of the services of their national Church. Since the union of the Crowns in the seventeenth century Church of Scotland congregations have been found in different parts of the capital. Their number has now been reduced to two – St. Columba's in Pont Street, Chelsea, and Crown Court in Covent Garden. St. Columba's, dating back to the opening of the eighteenth century, moved to its present site in 1884. The building then erected was destroyed by German fire bombs in 1941. Its successor, like Guildford Cathedral, was designed by Sir Edward Maufe and is a striking example of contemporary church architecture. The foundation stone was laid by Queen Elizabeth the Queen Mother in 1950 and the building completed in 1955. A generous response to the appeal from Scots all over the world, combined with war damage grants, enabled it to be constructed on a considerably larger scale, incorporating provision both for worship and for a wide range of congregational activities. In recent years the building has also formed a welcome centre for Scottish societies in the London area. The vision which inspired the planning of a church which could also function as a Christian community centre has been amply justified. London Scots are fortunate indeed to have this noble building calling them to worship in a sanctuary remarkable for its dignity, simplicity and serenity and enabling them to share meals together, to study and discuss, and, not least, to dance to well loved Scottish airs.

The strength of the congregation owes much to the inspired leadership of its ministers alike in the old building and the new.

Very senior members remember well Dr Archibald Fleming, gifted as church statesman, preacher and writer. Dr Fleming's colleague and successor, the Very Reverend R.F.V. Scott, led the congregation through the years of the Second World War. By the power of his preaching and the charm of his personality he held it together and inspired the efforts to raise the new church on the ashes of the old. The character of the present building owes much to his knowledge and the quality of his churchmanship. When Dr Scott retired early in 1960 I received a call from the congregation to be their minister.

I might well have wished to accept such an attractive invitation in any case; in the circumstances of Irene's death the move seemed a wise one. Bereavement is a challenge to a new beginning. In December 1960 Kenneth, Andrew and I left Scotland behind us with Sam, our Golden Labrador, to keep us company and ensure that our new home would not feel completely different from the old. We made the journey south by car, pulling a caravan heavy with our belongings. The weather was wintry with snow and ice most of the way. As we approached the northern outskirts of London thick fog descended. With some difficulty we crawled as far as Mill Hill and there decided to spend the night. By the following morning all was clear and we crossed London to our temporary abode in Kensington. With the hindsight I now possess the experience of our first twenty-four hours could be held to prefigure the course of events to come. There were to be times when the path ahead would be totally obscured and it seemed the journey must be abandoned. But the mists did clear and the journey was resumed.

With no sense of storms ahead we settled comfortably in the hotel which was to be our home until the manse adjacent to the church was ready. Comfortably is a misnomer as far as Sam was concerned. Hotel regulations meant that he had to live in the car until he won the heart of the manageress and was allowed to move in too. The boys found places in Latymer Upper School and all four of us received a kindly welcome from the large and widely dispersed congregation drawn from the greater London area and even further afield.

It was an exciting experience to work in such a setting, unique in so many ways. You go upstairs to church, unless you use the lift which serves the building from the lower hall level through four floors to the tower chapel or columbarium in which cremation caskets are laid up. From that point the journey to the top of the tower has to be made on foot. Accommodation is provided for a resident church officer and for a deaconess, when I arrived Miss Frances Danskin, long to be remembered in St. Columba's. In addition a guest flat is available for our visitors. This additional accommodation has been made possible by a most generous gift from Margaret, the widow of our beloved elder Dr Hubert Dunn. The building hummed with activity from morning till night. The church office dealt with an ever growing volume of mail and phone calls. Well appointed halls and kitchen premises on two levels made it possible to follow morning service on Sunday with a congregational lunch and provide catering facilities for the varied activities. We could claim to be in business seven days a week. No minister could have had a greater challenge or a more promising start.

Challenge was uppermost in my thoughts. St. Columba's was obviously booming. The congregation was at its peak. It couldn't be more 'successful'. Could it, perhaps, be even friendlier, homelier? At all events that would be my aim. If the congregation on Sunday was to be more of a family we needed a creche so that parents of young children could come to church together if they wished. If children were to feel the church belonged to them as much as to the adults then we ought to find a place in the service for a talk to the children before they left for Sunday School. Unless Baptisms took place during the course of the service the meaning of the Sacrament would be obscured. The child or adult is being received into the fellowship of the whole Church of which the local congregation is the representative, not just the family and friends. This could lengthen the service and at times create something of a disturbance but that's how it is with a real family. We needed a Bible Class if the needs of the fourteen to seventeen age groups were to be looked after. The creche is now taken for granted as are Baptisms during the service. The Bible Class, renamed the Senior Study Group, functions in close connection with the Sunday School.

On the debit side Sunday morning attendances in my days were smaller than they used to be. Dr Scott possessed outstanding gifts as a popular preacher. His eloquence plus the excitement of the splendid new building built morning congregations to mammoth proportions. In the fifties St. Columba's became famous as the church to which you must come early if you wanted a seat. This tradition was continued during the early years of my ministry when evening congregations also were comparatively large, but as the sixties gave place to the seventies, numbers declined. This, of course, is a cause of concern and disappointment to any preacher who, not unnaturally, takes any fall in attendance as a reflection of his own performance. I must certainly take my full share of the blame. In addition to its minister however, St. Columba's had problems enough. In a well populated suburban parish a lively congregation may still expect to maintain or increase its members. In the town, certainly in cases of a 'gathered' congregation like our own, with no parish allotted to it, the battle with the forces inimical to church attendance is more rarely won.

Exception must be made in the case of those congregations accepted as 'Evangelical'. Attendances there go from strength to strength. They are to be found within the Church of Scotland, the Church of England and denominations outside the so-called main line Churches. Like the Charismatic groups, with which they often have a good deal in common, they constitute the main Christian growing point in our day.

Surely this is to be welcomed, even if certain reservations must be made. Christian growing points are urgently needed and the mainline Churches no less urgently require the challenge the 'Evangelicals' present. Their worship and indeed their whole life are Bible centred. It is made clear that a Christian must know Jesus as his or her personal Saviour and reveal the fact by joy in worship and daily faithfulness in discipleship. Of course you can say this again of members of mainline congregations not classified as 'Evangelical'. They all contain men and women for whom Jesus indeed is Lord and the Word of God is authoritative; men and women who give sacrificially for the cause of Christ and the needs of their fellow men. In any of the mainline Churches, however, they may well be in the minority. The strength of an 'Evangelical' congregation is found in the concentration of the like minded. For the majority in the mainline Churches membership means much less in personal commitment and so yields much less in blessing.

The source of the Reformation has been found in praying groups throughout Europe. Here is a call to fervent Christian believers of any denomination, ministers and laymen alike, to pray for revival where they are, no matter how cold and lifeless the conventional congregation may appear to be. Prayer is needed no less for the 'Evangelicals', that the fullness of the Christian faith may inform their enthusiasm and enrich their Bible study.

Labels too often are libels. No congregation has any right to be called Christian if its character fails to be evangelical in the sense that the good news of the Gospel of Jesus Christ dominates its life and witness. Certainly we coveted the designation in St. Columba's and sought to be more worthy of it. Despite a reduction in membership there was real joy in our worship and real warmth in our fellowship. The range of congregational activities was wide indeed. The generosity of one of our members, the late Miss Park Lyle, provided Lyle Park, an Eventide Home in Putney. Ownership has now passed from the Church which still exercises pastoral concern for the residents. The well loved Bina Gardens Hostel which had long served the needs of young ladies coming to London eventually closed when flat sharing became the fashion. St. Columba's can be proud of its record of service for old and young alike in Lyle Park and Bina Gardens. Activities of a more domestic order were lively too. Sunday was always a sociable day with substantial numbers of worshippers waiting for lunch. The meal, provided by teams of volunteers, both men and women, is a very real help to those who travel long distances by car or bus or train to worship in what they feel is a bit of Scotland. It enabled us also to give a welcome to the visitors from Australia and New Zealand, the United States and other parts of our own country whose numbers showed no signs of declining. A visit to the church any Monday evening was likely to disclose a group from the Youth Fellowship at supper after their weekly prayers, a meeting of Alcoholics Anonymous, the odd committee meeting and a hallful of enthusiastic Scottish country dancers. Another evening would reveal a similar pattern, with one or other of the Scottish societies arranging the dancing and Scouts, badminton, Bible Study Group, sharing the available accommodation. One of my gifted assistants, Bruce McNicol, now minister of Jedburgh, confessed that while still in Glasgow he thought of his future assignment in London in terms of taking teas with Duchesses. We had indeed one such to our credit, and a very charming one at that. My colleagues and I would gladly have taken tea with the Duchess of Hamilton as often as permitted. In fact the workaday world of St. Columba's left little time for such pleasures, even when available.

I suppose the image of St. Columba's as a relic of Victorian 'Upstairs', where it still exists, is nurtured by the more high-powered of our weddings and the steady stream of memorial services for men and women who have made their mark on our national life. The list of these services through the years makes fascinating reading. Speaker of the House, Lord 'Shakes' Morrison, oil pioneer Lord Strathalmond and, much too soon afterwards, his son William, to name only a few. As I listened to the tributes paid to so many of my fellow countrymen and sought myself to compose them, I was left in no doubt that Scotland's most important export is still her sons and daughters.

This impression gathers strength as I reflect on my former flock. It is less star-studded than was the case in earlier days when Earls and Lords and Knights coveted a place on the Kirk Session. When Lord Reith, a regular worshipper with us in his London days, retired to Scotland his departure signalled the end of an era in which the 'establishment' rated institutional religion highly and were not slow to identify themselves with it. It is all the more remarkable that so many London Scots from so many varied spheres still accord the church of their fathers a special place in their affections. The occupations of most of our members were professional and their social background middle-class. If a stratified view of society is to be taken then they belonged to the very stratum on which the future of our country must largely depend. Will that future be Christian? As we worshipped together Sunday by Sunday and shared in Christian concern and service day by day we made our contribution to the answer.

It is said that if two Englishmen are landed on a desert island they will refuse to speak unless introduced. Two Welshmen in similar circumstances will certainly organise an Eistedfodd while two Irishmen will quickly come to blows. Two Scots without doubt will organise a Caledonian Society. London provides convincing evidence. Caledonian Societies abound in

all the suburbs while in central London Scottish community life
pursues a vigorous course. Members of St. Columba's played
their full part in the Royal Scottish Corporation, the oldest
Scottish charity in London. For some twenty years our elder,
the late Sir Edward Reid, Chairman of Barings Bank and
grandson of Queen Victoria's Scottish doctor, was the inspiration and the driving force in the life of the Royal Caledonian
Schools, founded after the Napoleonic wars as a home for
children of service families. The Caledonian Society of London, promoting fellowship among London Scots and their
guests, is pledged to the support of both Corporation and
Schools. Members and adherents of St. Columba's continued to
swell its ranks and not infrequently provided the leadership.
The Caledonian Club continues to prosper in a day when
Clubland has a struggle to survive. It provides an important
social centre for London Scots and their compatriots on their
visits south. The minister of St. Columba's is normally a member and, as I can testify, receives a very gracious welcome from
Club members whether or not belonging to his flock.

Congregational links with the London Scottish Regiment are
particularly precious. In recent years three of our elders,
Duncan Bennet, Gordon Maxwell and Jock Anderson, have
held the post of Regimental Colonel. No part of the church is
more used than the very beautiful London Scottish Chapel. No
church parade meant more to us than that of the Regiment each
Remembrance Sunday when veterans of both World Wars
march with their younger comrades of the Territorial Army
today. Every good Regiment develops its own family spirit, but
certainly none can rival that experienced at the London Scottish
Hallowe'en dinner. Our association with the Royal British
Legion is of a very personal kind as the Founder, Earl Haig, was
an elder in St. Columba's. The Earl Haig Branch of the Legion
parades to St. Columba's each year in thankful remembrance of
the Legion's founder. It is the privilege of the Minister of St.

Columba's to be as Chaplain to the Corporation, as also to the London Scottish. His circle of friendships is thus extended far beyond the bounds of the congregation.

Like any other London church which is open most of the time, St. Columba's received a steady stream of men and sometimes women in search of some contribution towards their support until their next social security payment was due. In a few cases they were professional 'con' men whose stories tended to have a familiar ring. Like plots for novels, the number available was strictly limited. In most cases the visitors were quite obviously down on their luck and much in need of any help they could get. Drink was often the problem but more frequently the man was singularly ill equipped, physically or mentally or both, for the demands life makes on us. Any help we could give in money or clothing was limited but an essential expression of concern for our fellow men. Information and advice sometimes met the case but both can appear cold and comfortless without some tangible token of sympathy. Just occasionally callers exhibited signs of a guilty conscience. I was pleasantly surprised one day when a poorly clad visitor, despite my protests, insisted on making a donation of two pounds to the church. It transpired that this had come from the wallet the contents of which he had appropriated from our downstairs cloakroom before our interview took place.

London is a Mecca for those trying to run away from life. Marriage breakdown is commonly the cause. A mother and her young son appeared on the church doorstep late one Saturday evening. They were looking for the husband who had left their home in Scotland in company with a lady friend. The two of them were believed to be together somewhere in London. What could we do to help? In this particular case our needle and haystack search succeeded and efforts to effect a reconciliation proved successful. The husband went home to make a new start in his marriage. His companion found work in

London and a place for herself in the life of St. Columba's. Efforts to find happy solutions to matrimonial problems often proved fruitless but there was always some way in which the difficulties of those concerned could be shared. They had a place in our daily prayers and we had reason often enough to thank God for the measure in which He used St. Columba's for the healing of human relationships and the preservation of homes threatened with disaster.

As public opinion changed and the use of the 'pill' increased, there were fewer cases of girls who had run away from home to have their babies in London. One such instance was quite unique. The young lady was only seventeen. She established herself in a bed-sitter in one of the poorer quarters and there she gave birth to her child on her own, without any assistance whatsoever. Something at least of the nature of her ordeal can be imagined. She didn't know where to look for help when she arrived in London and was too nervous to enquire. She was determined to be independent of the child's young father and to stand on her own feet. There was to be no marriage of necessity. Somehow or other she would look after herself and the child. A kind and concerned neighbour brought in the social services and they informed us that the girl would like to see a Church of Scotland minister. We were able to find suitable accommodation for mother and child. The father came down from Scotland and plans were made for the marriage which both parties very much wanted. In due course the baby was baptised and both parents took their share in the ceremony. An especially harrowing episode had a hopeful ending.

How grateful I am for the help of colleagues in these and countless other instances. On his retirement from his last parish the late Dr George Cameron, one of Scotland's most distinguished ministers, accepted my invitation to be associate minister. For five years I had the benefit of his companionship and counsel and St. Columba's enjoyed his devoted care. Our Deaconess for a like period was Tess Forsyth, who immediately won a place in our hearts she will never lose. The assistant ministers who year by year strengthened the team gave splendid service.

Much as I had looked forward to working in St. Columba's, I knew when I came south that a Church of Scotland charge in England would necessarily present its own problems. The Church of Scotland is presbyterian and presbyterian congregations abound in England. Are they to be bypassed just because they are English? It is true that English Presbyterians have now made common cause with Congregationalists to form the United Reformed Church. Nevertheless those congregations formerly presbyterian continue on their way with little modification. As far as ways of worship are concerned any congregation of the United Reformed Church is unlikely to feel all that different from the average parish church in Scotland. The Church of Scotland is the national church and its establishment does mean that it is different in character and feel from the English Free Churches. The question must still be asked whether we are Scots first and Christian second. If this is so it makes nonsense of the claim of the Christian Church to be the great reconciler and unifier of our divided world, not to mention the affirmation of Scripture that in Jesus Christ differences of race and nation are transcended. In a day of growing ecumenical concern are Church of Scotland congregations in England really an anachronism?

The question gains more point as the position of the Church of England changes. Until recently there was a very real bar to the participation of members of the Church of Scotland in the life of the local Anglican church. We could worship there if we chose but were only officially welcomed to communion if we were out of reach of the ministrations of our own church. This ruling no longer obtains. Any member of the Church of Scotland who receives communion in his own congregation may now receive it in the Church of England. If a member of the

Church of Scotland wishes to be enrolled in the Church of England it is still necessary to be confirmed according to the Anglican rite. Short of this the Scot in England may take a full and active part in the life of the church in his parish.

At their conference in Nottingham in 1964 those churches participating – all the main denominations in Britain except the Roman Catholics – affirmed their desire actively to seek union. This has now been further affirmed, by the Roman Catholics also, at the Swanwick Conference in August 1987. If we in the Church of Scotland are to pay more than lip service to such an aim, long since affirmed in our own constitution, we must encourage rather than discourage our members to affirm their oneness with their fellow Christian in every way they can. We are hardly likely to do this if we imply that there has to be a Church of Scotland congregation before a Scot may properly be expected to worship God.

Both our London congregations are strongly identified with Christians in their own areas. St. Columba's took an active part in the formation of the Chelsea Council of Churches. Ministers, whether Anglican, Roman or Free Church, were welcomed to our pulpit as I was to theirs. During the Week of Prayer for Christian Unity in 1963 a United service was held in St. Columba's in which for the first time members of the two local Roman Catholic Churches were allowed by their authorities to share. The church was packed and ministers of all the local communities concerned took part. When the service ended most people waited for tea and there was a marked unwillingness to disperse. I shook hands with the congregation when eventually they decided to leave and I have never known so many worshippers to be so moved. This was especially the case with our Roman Catholic guests for whom it was an entirely new experience to worship with fellow Christians in a church other than their own. For many of us at that moment the ecumenical movement became alive at the grass roots as it had never done at the great world congresses. In Chelsea as elsewhere we still very largely go it alone in our separate denominational lives, but the area of united Christian action grows steadily.

Whatever the ecumenical future may be, St. Columba's at present has an essential role to play. The Annual Scottish Festival service each St. Andrew's-tide, when Scots converge on St. Columba's from far and wide to worship together and hear a sermon from the Moderator of the year, suggests the cathedral type of ministry which both St. Columba's and Crown Court may exercise. It is proper that those who share a national heritage and national characteristics should have opportunity to commend their own country to God and to give thanks for the place in national life which the Kirk continues to hold for the welfare of Scotland and the wider world to which Scots continue to make their own special contribution. It is right also that the Church of Scotland should show its concern for Scots in London. Such an outpost of the Kirk need not conflict with the ecumenical spirit which should characterise every branch of the Church. St. Columba's is summoned like every other congregation so to order its life and relationship with fellow Christians as to hasten the day when the Church in any or all of its parts will be known and seen to be one.

On a September Sunday morning in the year 1966 members of the congregation of St. Columba's arriving for morning service were surprised to find newspaper posters strategically placed at the entrance to the church. I cannot recall the wording but they indicated a controversy involving the minister. There were copies of a Sunday paper on sale nearby which carried an article for all interested to read. A number of worshippers were so incensed that by the time the service was over the offending notices and papers were nowhere to be seen.

It wasn't the kind of publicity I would have chosen to announce my return to duty after a brief honeymoon in the

Algarve, but I can't say the incident was entirely unexpected. For some time before our marriage took place both my fiancée and I had been hounded by one particular reporter in what seemed to us a most distasteful and infuriating manner.

Of course there was a story, as the article to which I have referred made perfectly plain. It can be told quite briefly. In the month of November 1963 I conducted the funeral of a Colonel Keith Briant. As a result I became acquainted with his widow, Ruth. She subsequently became a member of the congregation and before many months had passed we both decided that we would wish to be married if we could. 'If' was the operative word. Before her marriage to Keith Briant Ruth had been married and divorced. Her husband by the earlier marriage was still alive. I knew that by Church of Scotland law it was possible for us to be married in church. I also knew that the marriage of a minister to a divorcee would not be well received by some members of the congregation. It might become impossible for me to continue in the ministry. Had I the right to abandon what I had always believed to be my calling?

I took my problem with me to hospital where I was due for an operation. No light was granted to me there. The longer Ruth and I pondered the situation the more insoluble it seemed. We had arranged to visit Scotland and were to leave on a Sunday morning. Before doing so I attended early communion at the nearby Parish Church. As I walked home from the service I thought I heard God speak within my heart. 'You are to be married,' I thought He said, 'and you are to remain in the ministry.'

Was it really the voice of God? Was it wishful thinking of the most obvious and naive description? I supposed that only time would tell. I knew that I could not rule out the possibility that it had indeed been the voice of God. The problem we faced had not been uppermost in my mind as I went to church. I wanted primarily to thank God for His care over me in hospital. The operation had involved a good deal of pain and discomfort. I wanted to thank God for enabling me to bear it all without making too much of a nuisance of myself. I wanted to commend to God our journey north and to place our whole family circle and my work in His hands. The message which had come to me appeared to come unsought. I thanked God for it at the time. How much more I was to thank Him in the days which followed.

The message from God, if it was really such, was in my thoughts as we drove north. In competition with a Siamese cat protesting loudly in the back seat and a patient Labrador occupying too much space under the dashboard, I tried to think through yet again the issues raised for the Christian by divorce. I had always felt divorce to be one of the ultimates in human tragedy. Blessed in my own marriage, in my wife and sons, so far beyond all my deserving, the sanctities of home meant more than ever. Little wonder that I was desperately afraid to act in any way that seemed to belie my cherished belief. Little wonder that the very word 'divorce' struck a chill within my heart.

Our journey to Scotland included a visit to Edinburgh which houses the headquarters of the Church of Scotland. One of the senior officials there was a man I knew well enough to consult on my problem. He took the down-to-earth pragmatic view that all would depend on the way in which our marriage, if it took place, was received by my congregation. He advised me to sound out some of my office-bearers. If their reaction was favourable he felt I could assume the congregation as a whole would also take a favourable view. Back in London I put the advice into practice and found, to my surprise, that those consulted raised no objections. We assumed we could plan for a wedding date, but no sooner had we started to do so than news reached us that in certain quarters of the congregation the strongest criticism of our proposed marriage was, in fact, being expressed. We were back where we started and agreed to make no further plans until the position should be clearer.

Nightmare is not too strong a word for the experience of the months which followed. I was convinced that God had called me to the ministry and despite my unworthiness had blessed my work and was blessing it still. Reports of opposition to our marriage reawakened all my fears that this would be inconsistent with my calling and that I must choose one or the other. I had known fear in wartime days as at other times. I had known the agony of bereavement. This was a new kind of misery, the misery of uncertainty, the dread that any path I chose might lead to evil; that all the paths to good were somehow closed.

In the Church of Scotland it is our custom to have Communion for the whole congregation on certain Sundays of the year. In St. Columba's Easter Day is one of these. Before the crowded day was over my period of uncertainty had ended. It came home to me, as I believed, that we were meant to marry and that I must lay my plans accordingly. I felt equally sure that this would mean the end of my work as a parish minister and that I must find some other work consistent with my calling.

My father, whose sense of humour never deserted him, used to observe that when in this life one door closes another shuts. I was now to experience this in a big and painful way. None of the avenues it seemed reasonable to explore led anywhere. My *amour propre*, over-fortified through the years by more success than I probably deserved, took some nasty knocks. As no paid employment was in sight I decided to try to earn my living by writing. I had one small book to my credit and some experience at least of religious journalism. It was little enough, but I had to do something. We started to look for somewhere to live and I pondered a suitable date on which to resign my charge. It was now the summer of 1965 and I felt that I should not leave on the eve of another session's work. I decided to send my letter of resignation in the following May, and this I did.

Thereafter events followed a course I could certainly not have foreseen. The Presbytery, the court of the Church to which as a minister I am subject, followed its usual course and upon the receipt of my letter appointed a small committee to meet me. As a result of our conference I felt led to withdraw my resignation. Simultaneously a group of my office-bearers, learning of my attempted resignation, urged me to get married and stay on as minister. I took their advice. On 26th August we were married in the Church of Greyfriars in Edinburgh. It now seemed that the voice I had heard in my heart a year ago had indeed been the voice of God.

I have referred to the publicity we received on our first Sunday back on duty. If the organisers hoped thereby to increase our problems their aim was not achieved. Members went out of their way to wish us well and in due course a congregational social to welcome us both was arranged by our senior elder, Mr James Steele, and his wife. The difficulties did not immediately vanish, but in every case known to us enmity and suspicion gave place to trust and goodwill. It is becoming difficult for me now to remember that even for a brief period the position was ever different.

I have no wish to suggest that those who were our critics were wrong-headed or ill intentioned. We were ourselves only too conscious of the different views which might be taken and the seeming and painful impossibility of being sure that what we planned was right. As often as I recall the period of uncertainty and strain I am moved to renewed thankfulness for the strength I believe we were given and the reality of the guidance of God which I believe may be discerned. It was especially agonising for me to think that my ties with my people might be broken. In the goodness and mercy of God they were preserved and, as it seems to me, strengthened. We had moving and indeed overwhelming evidence of this when in 1986 the time came for me to retire. Before that time arrived, however, the

invitation to be Moderator of the General Assembly of the
Church of Scotland resulted in a year's leave of absence and one
of the most fascinating and enjoyable years of my life.

Chapter 11

Moderator of the General Assembly

'You'll enjoy being Moderator,' a former holder of the office wrote to me when I was nominated. 'There's nothing like it.' It is certainly true that the Moderator is not an executive. He doesn't hire or fire. He is not a Presbyterian Pope or Archbishop. He is not head of the Church of Scotland. He, and perhaps some day it may be she, is a minister like any other who, after nomination by a Committee representative of the whole Church and approved by the General Assembly, is released from normal duty for one year to undertake special responsibilities. These fall into two unequal parts. Immediately on appointment by the General Assembly he is called upon to act as Moderator, i.e. as Assembly Chairman or Speaker. Thereafter he visits the Church, at home and abroad, as requested. For this year of office he acts as the official representative of the Kirk.

Although the Assembly now lasts for only seven days the Moderator's responsibilities are demanding. This is the Kirk's parliament – the only one, so far, that Scotland can claim for itself. The life and work of the Church are reviewed. Policies are debated by some fifteen hundred men and women, half of them ministers and half elders, drawn from every part of Scotland and most walks of life. If this example of Christian democracy is to work then the agreed rules of procedure and debate

must be kept and a fair deal given to all. What has impressed me
through the years, as it did again when I surveyed the scene
from the Chair, is the kindliness and patience of all present
when someone, clearly unaccustomed to public speaking, found
the courage to express some real concern. An obvious change
of mood could be easily discerned in the case of the speaker too
much at home and too little aware of the passage of time. Like
most if not all of my predecessors, I had contemplated my
Assembly responsibilities with some trepidation. In the event I
found it a thrilling and happy experience. As we began each day
with our brief act of worship, joining in the unaccompanied
singing of the Metrical Psalms – an experience as unforgettable
as it is moving – and as we gathered at the Lord's Table to take
the Bread and the Wine and to receive our Saviour we found a
unity which sustained us through the hours of discussion and
blessed us with a comradeship strong enough to take the strain
of difference in points of view. His predecessors are at hand to
release the serving Moderator from the Chair whenever necessary and the Convener of the Business Committee, along with
the Procurator, are standing by to help when guidance for the
Chair is required. How grateful I was for the assurance that if
on any occasion I failed to do much good at least I would
quickly be restrained from doing too much harm!

When the Queen is not present she sends her representative,
the Lord High Commissioner, who, for the period of the
Assembly, holds court in Holyrood Palace, and is accorded all
the honour due to Her Majesty. Sir John Gilmour occupied this
position in 1983 and how splendidly he and his lady fulfilled
their duties. Sir John's presence was a symbol of the Establishment of the Church of Scotland just as his occupancy of the
gallery above and apart from the floor spoke of the Church's
freedom from State control. The Holyrood Garden Party to
which Sir John invited the Assembly and the entertainment
of distinguished guests in the Palace brought colour to the

Assembly, the latter linking Assembly proceedings with the whole life of the nation. By custom the Moderator and his lady give their own Reception – in our case in the beautiful Signet Library, so graciously granted. An effort is made to make the guest list as representative as possible of the different areas of the Kirk's concern. We were specially glad to welcome the 'backroom' ladies and gentlemen whose tasks in the Church Offices may at times lack glamour but never importance.

I would be less than honest if I failed to admit that the Assembly, making demands on every working hour and not a few required for sleeping, proved taxing in the extreme. How grateful Ruth and I were for the Residence now at the Moderator's disposal throughout the year in the Georgian House in Charlotte Square, and for the limousine which ensured that we got to our right place at the right time. Of course it was not all work and no play. How much we enjoyed our stay in Holyrood and how kindly we were entertained by the Edinburgh City Fathers and Mothers in their Chambers. Nevertheless it was reassuring at times to reflect that for each Moderator there is only one Assembly Week. The months that lay ahead would no doubt hold their own privileges and problems but at least these would be less highly concentrated.

The Moderator is required to visit a number of presbyteries and to spend ten days in each. These are planned well in advance by the Assembly Clerk on whose counsel and help the Moderator continually leans heavily and gratefully. A tribute must be paid also to the Assistant to the Clerk, Miss Chris Brown, to whom each Moderator owes the greatest debt. A presbytery may expect to receive a Moderatorial visit once in ten years and the visit is greatly valued. The form varies little. On the two Sundays the Moderator preaches at the maximum number of services, often joint, which can be arranged, meeting those present at Receptions following. On weekdays he addresses rallies of the Woman's Guild and Office-bearers'

Unions. Church meetings however occupy by no means the greater part of the tour. The Christian faith is concerned with the seven days of the week and not Sunday only. The Moderator visits schools, colleges, hospitals, prisons, Police, factories, fish farms, shipyards. The ten days of each visit could not conceivably be fuller.

Presbytery visits could hardly have had a more romantic beginning than that supplied by Lochcarron and Skye. A train journey from Edinburgh to Kyle of Lochalsh, via Inverness, carried us through some of Scotland's loveliest country in unbroken sunshine. For Ruth and for me Skye was new territory and how thrilled we were to set foot on it. The five days spent in Sligachan Hotel passed much too quickly but allowed us full opportunity to meet islanders as they worshipped and worked in a setting which never lost its magic. Our days on the mainland were equally memorable and yielded a special bonus when we visited the Gardens at Inverewe and wondered at their beauty. Church life has its own problems in such areas but rejoices still in an understanding of its relevance by the whole community much harder to find in busy townships. The care with which we were shepherded throughout by the Presbytery Clerk, the Reverend Allan Macarthur, was as unceasing as it was kind.

Paisley Presbytery provided a vivid and no less fascinating contrast. I proved to be the fourth Moderator for whom the Presbytery Clerk, the Reverend William Bell, had cared, in each case with the same thought and efficiency. If I call it the Caring Presbytery this is not to imply that others are uncaring but simply that the description so quickly forced itself upon me. Paisley Christian Social Action Centre, led with such infectious enthusiasm by the Reverend Thomas Cant, is a tribute to the love and vision of a great and increasingly ecumenical Christian company. Much of our time was spent with the disabled, both young and old, so admirably tended by schools and hospitals.

Paisley provided also the opportunity to witness the ministry of the Police to the whole community, one too often lacking recognition and appreciation. Police concerns are by no means limited to the control of crime. Much of their time and effort, in Paisley as elsewhere, goes into the work of Community Relations and the endeavour to help young people to replace drugs with healthier interests. Our visit to the Police ended with a conducted tour of Paisley in a police car and a glimpse of areas in which social problems are at their most acute. How much our parish ministers there need our prayers as they strive to build a strong and compassionate Christian fellowship in the midst of vandalism, violence, unemployment and squalor.

If I had been looking for another vivid contrast, the Presbytery of Dunoon provided it in the month of January. Weather reports assumed a new and urgent interest for me as I joined the Rothesay Ferry at Wemyss Bay. The snow was falling quickly and the ferry rolled from side to side in a highly undisciplined and unfriendly fashion. I wondered how impassable the roads of Bute would prove. The Presbytery Clerk, the Reverend Ronald Samuel, was on the pier to greet and reassure me. There proved to be no special problems if I discount the afternoon service in Ascog where the organ would have played and light and heat have been supplied had the gale not severed the power connection the night before.

That apart I was able to carry through the full Bute programme of visits arranged by the Regional Council. When however the time came to move to Cowal plans had to be changed. Weather dictated a crossing from Rothesay to Wemyss Bay and another from Gourock to Hunters Quay to resume my duties. Deep snow then curtailed them and long planned events had unfortunately to be cancelled. However meetings of the Presbyterial Council of the Woman's Guild and the Office-bearers' Union were held as well as an Ecumenical Evening Service well supported by local denominations.

Weather little kinder welcomed me to the Presbytery of Buchan. My desire to greet personally the seemingly endless stream of worshippers leaving Fraserburgh Old in what felt like a force ten gale rewarded me with a brief attack of bronchitis which for a day or two put a stop to my journeys but released an even stronger flow of the affectionate concern which envelops a Moderator as he travels. My host and hostess, the Reverend and Mrs Douglas Clyne, had me fit again very quickly and the Presbytery Clerk, the Reverend James Fraser, made the necessary adjustments for me. This compulsory pause allowed reflection on this corner of Scotland with its long established skills in agriculture, fishing and boat building to which are now added the demands and enrichments of the offshore industry. The linking of charges here, as almost universally elsewhere in rural Scotland, seriously reduces the number of ministers and calls for a fuller share in pastoral care by elders. This is apparently taken with enthusiasm and is reflected in the life of the community. In school and Council Chamber, in industry and commerce, the influence of the Christian Church is clearly evident.

Our ten days in the Presbytery of Stirling had the feel of a grand finale – not least because a splendid Rolls Royce had been placed at our disposal; only of course, I hasten to add, for the duration of our visit. This had been arranged through the good offices of the Very Reverend Dr Peter Brodie who, in company with the Presbytery Clerk, the Reverend Thomas Kinloch, had planned the whole visit with consummate care and his own characteristic skill. A highlight was the Reception so generously given by the Earl of Marr and Kellie in the splendid setting of the Castle, of which he is Hereditary Keeper. The civil service in the Holy Rude was equally memorable. The local cattle market afforded me the unusual opportunity of addressing the farmers, and any of their animals who happened to be listening at the time, from the auctioneer's 'pulpit'.

Moderators tend to travel the globe, or at least to any part of it where the Kirk is specially concerned. There were no exotic trips for me to China or Japan, India or Africa, but I have no reason to complain. Following our own General Assembly I flew to Dublin to attend that of the Presbyterian Church of Ireland, found on both sides of the Border. I listened to a moving appeal to our Queen for fuller protection of the residents of the Border areas of the North. I was to visit our Army in Northern Ireland later in the year and saw for myself the patience and resolution with which our service men and women seek to shield our fellow-citizens from savage and unrelenting attack at steadily mounting cost to themselves. Glib assertions that only religion is to blame for it all are challenged by the increasing co-operation of Protestant and Roman Catholic churchmen and the powerful witness of the Corymeela Community, founded by the Reverend Rae Davy, a fellow student of mine in New College. Those who bomb and maim to get the Brits out do so to further their political aim. It must be said that Ulster Protestants who have been less than fair to Roman Catholics in their midst have their own share of responsibility for the present tragic impasse and some at least of their number are not to be outdone in violence. I cannot have been the first, nor shall I be the last, visitor to the Province to acknowledge the apparent impossibility of seeing any solution fair to all parties. At least I could be certain that no satisfactory answer will ever be found without continuing and urgent prayer and without the peace-seeking presence of our Army, strengthened as it is both by the Police and the Territorials who regularly change civilian clothes for uniform and subject themselves by day and night to horrendous risks against which they can have little or no protection.

If I left Ireland with a proud and heavy heart my next assignment was one of unalloyed pleasure. Accompanied by the then Assembly Clerk, the Reverend Donald Macdonald, and

Elder Professor Kerrigan, I flew to join the two great American
Presbyterian Churches, separated since the days of the Civil
War, for their Uniting Assembly in Atlanta, Georgia. Our
welcome could not have been warmer and the local tempera-
tures followed suit. At least I enjoyed the shade of my tricorned
'Dick Turpin' hat. Professor Kerrigan wore full Highland cos-
tume. In a manner reminiscent of Edinburgh 1929 the two
Churches, after meeting separately to agree Union, converged
to march together to the City Hall, led, incidentally, by Pipes
and Drums. Along with the Moderators of the two Churches
your own Moderator marched, along with his kilted companion, both of us losing pounds in the blazing sun, thanks to our
unyielding garments. In due course I was invited to address the
united Assembly and to convey the greetings of our own and to
express our prayers for our Presbyterian brethren in the States,
so greatly strengthened by their union and so potent a force for
our Lord in a country so decisive in influence in our tragically
divided world.

Germany was next on the list of our overseas calls, occasioned
by the quincentenary celebrations of the birth of Martin
Luther. Memories came flooding back as I set foot on German
soil at Köln after some forty years. I can still remember how
strange it felt then to step from the freedom and sanity of life in
Edinburgh into a country that was, in effect, one vast prison
camp where those Jews as yet not rounded up went in terror of
their lives, where all the organs of the media poured out non-
stop vicious Nazi propaganda, where truth and justice were
systematically trampled under foot. How different the situation
had become. A new democracy has been born and without any
doubt today is alive and well. The Church and every other
institution is free. Neither Jew nor Gentile need have any fear
of the State. This transformation has been achieved, as so much
else, by the Allied victory at a cost we never dare forget. My
journey in West Germany took me first to Bonn where I spent a

very delightful evening with the British Ambassador and his wife, Sir John and Lady Taylor. From Bonn to Worms of Diet fame where the Evangelical Church of Germany was holding its annual Synod, the equivalent of our General Assembly. Martin Luther was in everyone's thoughts but the subject on which discussion and controversy centred was the deployment of the missiles on German soil. A strong rejection had come from the Reformed Churches included within the national Evangelical Church which also comprises Lutheran and so-called United – a combination of Lutheran and Reformed Churches, the Reformed being more akin to the Church of Scotland. The Synod refused to adopt the Reformed rejection as national Church policy but committed itself to continuing discussion. This debate over what is known as the Peace Question was much in evidence throughout West Germany as in East.

Cross to the East and you entered a different world. First the struggle to obtain a visa in time and then the passage, often delayed, through Checkpoint Charlie. It was my first glimpse of the cruel Wall, symbol of the gulf between two nations meant to be one. Little did I think that so soon and so drastically it would be breached. Of course the situation in East Germany was not the same as that which obtained in the whole country under Nazi rule but there were far too many disquieting reminders. There was the same attempt to brainwash the nation, concentrating on the young. The Christian faith was seen as the enemy and treated as such. The path to further education and promotion was invariably blocked for the Christian. True that during this Luther year the State co-operated with the Church to arrange the celebrations but when the attention of the world no longer focused on the country it had to be anticipated that the Government would revert to its former politics and that the trials of our fellow-Christians would continue. They did and were endured to such good effect that when the people rose in protest they found a strong and active Church to welcome them.

In East Berlin I met leaders of the Evangelical Church of the Union before proceeding to Eisleben and Leipzig. The world had come to Eisleben to give thanks for Martin Luther where he was born and baptized. The market square, with the Luther statue in the centre, was thronged with men and women of many nations and many branches of the Christian Church. A moving moment followed the series of addresses. The local Lutheran pastor and the local Roman Catholic priest together carried the Cross to the base of the statue and each in turn led us in prayer. In Leipzig great services of thanksgiving united representatives of the worldwide Church in thanksgiving for the great Reformer.

At the suggestion of one of our Euro-MPs I next visited Strasbourg. One day is hardly sufficient to absorb and assess this new political animal. Angry noises off, as French farmers staged one of their typical rallies, perhaps injected a note of realism into the proceedings. How near and yet so far, perhaps sums up my feelings as I rejoiced to see evidence of increasing European co-operation and at the same time could not fail to mark that political blood continues to be thicker than national water.

Two overseas tours still remained. A second visit to Germany was devoted in the main to the Army. I met with the Royal Scots Dragoon Guards, the Black Watch and the Gordons and I spent a no less fascinating day with the RAF in Bruggen. The manning of the 'front line' in conditions of the somewhat fragile peace between the Great Powers is as demanding as it is essential. Our representatives, whether on the ground or in the air, do us as much credit as anyone knowing our Services would expect. Thank God that the peace which is their aim seems less fragile now.

My last tour was the most fleeting and as enjoyable as, in a sense, it was superficial. I was requested by the Board of World Mission and Unity to convey greetings, in the Martin Luther quincentenary year, to the Lutheran Churches in Finland, Sweden, Norway and Denmark. If the time in each capital had to be short I was certainly not denied the kindest of welcomes from the Church leaders in each centre. It was clear the feeling of deep and essential unity was strong. I was privileged indeed to rejoice in its warmth.

It would seem that a Moderator's post-Assembly programme resembles the traditional sermon. It has three parts. Part one is given to presbyteries, part two to overseas travel and part three to anything and everything else he may be invited to do on the home front. The third part proved not one whit less interesting than the first two. I find myself thinking of individual congregations whose life, at least for a few hours, I was invited to share. Anniversary celebrations were usually the reason. They ranged from Torosay on the Isle of Mull to St. Columba's in London where the Queen was Guest at the service to mark the centenary of the move of the congregation to Pont Street. St. Columba's, Aberdeen, certainly qualifies for special mention. It was planned and built by both the Church of Scotland and the Roman Catholic Church. It is in three inter-connected sections. At one end there is a church for the Church of Scotland, at the other end one for the Roman Catholic Church and in between an area in which the two congregations can and do meet. The creation of this joint venture is a tribute to the minister and Session of St. Machar's Cathedral and the Roman Catholic Bishop of Aberdeen who have long worked together in trust and love. What a pleasure and privilege it was to share in the dedication of the whole building with Cardinal Gray.

It was my great good fortune to be Moderator in the year when the Boys' Brigade celebrated its centenary. I shall long remember the scene in Ibrox Park when some fifty thousand BB members, past and present, assembled to enjoy an Exhibition of BB activities which could hardly be surpassed. The same number gathered on the Sunday for a service at which I was invited to preach. I had to confess that I was really a Scout in

BB clothing but my vast congregation made it clear that would be overlooked – for once!

How many were my privileges – to take the Salute at the Edinburgh Tattoo, to enjoy the hospitality of Balmoral in company with the Queen, the Duke of Edinburgh and Princess Margaret plus the very special bonus of afternoon tea with our beloved Queen Mother in Birkhall. For me the annual Moderatorial visit to London was a particular pleasure. I saw a host of friends as I carried through the normal calls on leaders of Church and State. I believe I broke new ground by calling on Prime Minister Margaret Thatcher by whom I was most graciously received. I enjoyed the usual visit to the Houses of Parliament and the opportunity to preach, in the Crypt, at the Service for Scottish Peers and Members of Parliament. At the Royal Smithfield Show I was invited to present the prizes but not, I am thankful to say, to assist the judges. After some twenty-three years in London I was in very familiar territory but wearing, quite literally, a different hat. From time to time changes in the Moderatorial garb are considered. I am bound to say that in my opinion the present distinctive uniform is an ally no Moderator should wish to lose.

You could say I started my Moderatorial year with a formidable job description. The 'Urgent Call to the Kirk' invited the Moderator to lead the Kirk in prayer and intercession for a renewal of the Church and the conversion of Scotland in which some three million people remain to be won for Christ and His Church. 'The membership of the Kirk steadily diminishes,' states the Call. 'A damaging cut-back in churches and worshipping communities takes place: there are fewer and fewer pastors . . .' 'Facts are chiels that winna ding' and during my Moderatorial year these facts were never far from my thoughts. Nevertheless I was continually impressed and encouraged by the congregations I visited – by Ministers, Office-bearers, Sunday School teachers, Choir members, men and women in the pew. I found a joy in Christian worship among young and old alike and an enthusiasm for service to our fellow men. Those who belong to our slimmed down Church today would hardly be there without a sense of their own need and the need of the world for that fullness of life which only Christ can bestow. The anxiety and fear which few can long escape open ears and hearts to the Gospel message. What shall we do to be saved from the growing disunity in our own land and the cosmic disaster another world war must bring? Man's extremity, of which our people must be growing aware, is God's opportunity and that of the people called by His Son to His service. As I companied with so many who are hearing and answering that call little wonder that I ended my year with strengthened faith and deepened thankfulness and joy.

I learned too how strong are the links between Church and State in Scotland. The Church of Scotland is the National Church in more than name. Only one-third of the citizens of Scotland are on the roll of any Church and less than twenty per cent are on the roll of the Church of Scotland. Nevertheless the generous official welcomes I everywhere received from Regional and District Councils and the friendliness of the reception I everywhere encountered convinces me that the Kirk continues to possess a valued place in the life of Scotland. People look to it still with interest and expectancy. For this we certainly owe a great debt to ministers who serve as Chaplains to the Armed Services, to the Police, to hospitals, schools, universities and to industry. Thanks to their endeavours the Church goes out to those who in most cases do not come to the Church.

As I waited in the corridor of the Assembly Hall, with some degree of tension, to hear whether or not the Assembly would approve of my nomination, I knew that if it did I would face a year of unique experience and inestimable privilege. I knew also that I would not lack for companionship. My wife Ruth could not accompany me on my overseas tours but shared the presbytery visits in Scotland and the warm welcomes we everywhere received. In the Edinburgh Residence, when duties allowed us to be there, she proved as always the perfect hostess. Like my predecessors in office I learned how valuable and how valued is the role of the Moderator's Lady from the start of the crowded year to its close.

Chapter 12

Reluctant Retirer

When I was ordained to the Ministry in 1938 there was no compulsory retiring age. Short of committing some shocking and unfrocking offence and provided I remained in sufficient health I could not be removed from my charge unless I removed myself. Ministers of the Church of Scotland are inducted to a charge *ad vitam aut culpam* – for as long as they live (now until the prescribed retirement age) or until they are judged sufficiently culpable and removed on that score. Some years ago a Commissioner at the General Assembly, rather critical of the clergy, remarked ruefully that the trouble with ministers was 'too much *vitam* and not enough *culpam*'. Not short of *vitam* and judged to be clear of *culpam*, I had to decide the time to leave St. Columba's. After some twenty-six years I found this extremely hard to do. There was, in fact, nothing I wanted to do less. Of course I had been 'translated', as they say, on several occasions, but although I sorrowed each time to leave people who meant much to me and to whom I seemed to matter, there was the excitement and the challenge of a new chapter. No doubt retirement would be a challenge but could it be said to be exciting?

I knew I was more fortunate that many of my fellow ministers. On her death my mother had left me her home. This enabled me to keep level with rising house prices and ensured that we would have somewhere to live when I was no longer employed. As ministers of the Church of Scotland occupy tied houses and as their stipends are relatively low, their position when retirement comes along can be serious indeed. This is a problem to which as yet the Kirk has insufficiently addressed itself. I do not believe that inadequate salaries deprive the Church of the services of men and women who receive a strong call to the ministry. I am equally certain that every member of the Church has a duty to ensure that where the Church is an employer it discharges its responsibilities in a way that is fair to the employees. It is true that the General Assembly reveals a growing concern in this matter but there is urgent need of much more prayer and much more effort if material conditions for ministers and their wives and families are to be improved.

Ministers' salaries vary from church to church. Generally speaking the more affluent the congregation the higher the salary. A central fund, to which all congregations contribute according to their means, ensures a basic minimum in those cases where a congregation fails to do so. From time to time ministers and laymen criticise the present salary structure. Would it not be fairer, it is asked, both to ministers and congregations, if every minister enjoyed the same financial treatment? There could be an appropriate starting level and then increments to represent length of service and the special needs of particular appointments. Surely this would ensure, it is argued, that ministers would not be tempted to leave areas of deprivation for those in which higher rates are available. The argument seems very strong. A flat rate would emphasise the equal importance of the minister's task, irrespective of the district in which it might be performed. It would also suggest that the rewards of the minister's calling are to be found in the work itself. I doubt if our country is more materialistic in spirit than it used to be, although this is frequently asserted. It is certainly true that thanks to our economic recovery vast numbers of our people have never had it so good and young people have never had so much money at their disposal. Not unnaturally more and more of everything is demanded. A ministry clearly structured on a basis so different could bear a witness all the more effective by contrast. Such a claim may come ill from me since on each occasion when I was called to another congregation the salary was on a higher level. I am sure I was grateful for the increase. Lacking independent means, money or the lack of it loomed fairly large. On the other hand, what attracted me in each case was the challenge and the opportunities of the work to which I was being called. Had the salaries offered in Bearsden and St. Columba's been no larger than that paid in Broughty Ferry, I have no doubt I would have accepted the invitations offered to me. I wanted and welcomed more responsibility.

That in itself is no doubt legitimate enough but the other side of the coin may tell a different story. Welcoming what the world regards as a bigger job is hard to distinguish from the desire to be hailed as a bigger man. Certainly in my case the urge to 'get to the top' in one way or another has asserted itself from my earliest days. It apparently mattered a great deal that I should be captain of any team or first in any class. Failure to continue my early record of success in these respects in the closing school years seems to have taught me little. It continued to be of great importance to me that I became successively chairman of the Student Christian Movement University branch and President of the New College Missionary Union. Not that I resorted to any unfair means to secure my election but it mattered to me, much more than it should, that I was chosen for a leading role. As the years passed I have grown more conscious of the James Fraser McLuskey greater yet campaign and have asked God to help me to put and keep it in its place if it has any. It would be surprising if I had not wished to be Moderator, in a sense the highest place the Kirk affords.

That the invitation eventually came seemed to me, and will always seem, little short of miraculous. I had no doubt of my own inadequacies for the job and yet, with a fine disregard for logic, was sure it was something I could do. Several of those who wrote congratulating me on the appointment said they were pleased about it precisely because I was such a humble man. Unless they were all hopelessly wide of the mark humility can and does cohabit with ambition. If I lacked the necessary qualifications to justify the description of tycoon at least I never lacked the mentality.

I was loth to retire and leave St. Columba's because I revolted against the loss of what I and everyone else considered to be a top job. But I would be less than honest if I denied that people mattered to me just as much. I didn't want to leave so many men and women and children who made it clear they really didn't want me to go. You could say that people have always kept getting in the way. They have kept me from doing other things – reading, studying, working, playing. They have always seemed much more important than anything else. People, old and young, male and female, married and single, have made what I have always felt to be sovereign demands, taking priority over all else. This is specially the case when those concerned are in trouble but it is also true when they have joys to share. The other side of the coin is the reward of their trust and affection and this I have enjoyed in richest measure throughout my whole working life as a minister. Of course there have been exceptions but they have been so few and far between that it has always struck me as somewhat odd and just a little surprising when someone quite clearly was not enamoured of McLuskey and even went so far as to take a poor view of the man. With the passing of the years I have come to admit, however reluctantly, that they may have a point.

Whatever the job personal relationships play a vitally important role for good or ill. We are all dealing with other people in

one way or another. In the case of the minister, however, like
that of the family doctor, where he or she still exists, or the
social worker, other people dominate the scene most of the
time. They are not ousted by machinery which has to be tended
unceasingly, or buildings which have to be designed and
erected, or land which has to be farmed, or businesses which
have to be conducted, or any of the other multitudinous responsibilities which occupy the working hours of most of our
fellow men. Genuine concern for people, whoever they are, a
willingness to enter their lives when so invited, to share their
deepest needs, the capacity to remember them and their particular situations – all these are musts for anyone who would be
a minister sharing by His grace the role of the Good Shepherd.
By the same token, to part from one's flock is, as the French
have it, to experience a kind of death.

Withdrawal symptoms are no less acute when Sundays no
longer provide a pulpit. Of course the minister in retirement
may continue to preach when so invited but the weekly privilege and responsibility which have been his for so long are
suddenly removed. In one way it is a relief not to have the
recurring deadline to meet for some eleven months of the year.
The work involved in producing one sermon a week, if not
two, is considerable but then so is the satisfaction when there is
reason to believe that God has spoken His own Word to our
people as we ourselves have sought to hear and express it.

The message is not the preacher's but God's. God comes to
His own world in the Person of His Son Jesus Christ. That is
wonderful enough but not less so is the fact that He keeps
coming in a unique way to those who know Jesus as their
Friend and Saviour. In His words and deeds, in His death and
resurrection, God speaks to us here and now; challenging us to
see our own lives and the life of the world as He sees them;
challenging us to love as He loves. Not only does God challenge; He promises to enable us in His own strength to live

according to His will. Here then is the preacher's theme as it is
the theme of the Bible. With all due respect to Wordsworth,
the world cannot be too much with the preacher. God loved it
so much as to give His only Son. No sermon which sounds
remote from the world in which we live can be truly Christian,
nor can it claim that description unless an other-wordly note
sounds throughout. 'How great Thou art' is the triumph song
with which each sermon and each act of worship must ring: a
great God and a Saviour, equally in the twentieth century as in
the first.

In the nature of things a sermon is a performance and the
minister, for better or worse, a performer. Retirement means
withdrawing from the stage. When on it the minister must
speak so as to be easily heard. He must so comport himself as to
attract rather than distract. Must he read his discourse or refrain
from reading? There is no simple answer. A sermon may be
read so well and so unobtrusively as to constitute no barrier
between preacher and congregation. If the sermon content has
real value then reading at least ensures its delivery. On the other
hand, the preacher may feel, as I have come to do, that reading
a script keeps him from making as direct a personal contact with
the congregation as he would wish. In my case this feeling grew
with the years. Only in recent years did I decide to make more
time available for sermon preparation so that, after I had written
out the sermon in full, I could then reduce it to note form. This
exercise helped to get the sermon itself firmly into my head
while the notes, more or less extensive, could be at hand in the
pulpit to consult if necessary. Preparation of this kind is much
more demanding but the results from the point of view of
preacher and congregation appear as a rule much more rewarding. Certainly this has been my experience and I wish I had
made proof of this method at a much earlier stage in my
ministry. I do thank God that I was eventually led to this
approach to preaching and found it, for myself and for my

listeners, increasingly effective. It leads me to plead for the strongest possible emphasis to be placed on the technique of sermon preparation in our theological colleges. Content must not yield to technique but too often the reverse has been the case. As far as preaching is concerned both require equal attention. The Church of Scotland has yet to give adequate attention to instruction in the preaching art.

Of course it is not only as a preacher that the minister must learn to be a craftsman – and feel somewhat lost when there is no demand for his skill. Effectiveness in preaching encourages people to come to church but once there they have to be helped to worship. They may do so as the Bible is read, as well as preached, as they sing and as they pray. They may worship as they keep silence. In each respect appropriate aids are required and the minister must see that they are supplied. Readers drawn from the congregation and the discriminating use of modern versions can be a real strength. Hymns and metrical psalms should be such as enable the majority to sing freely and the congregational repertoire should be extended gradually but inexorably, perhaps with practices for the purpose or prior demonstration by the Choir. Prayers, which should never be too long, should speak not only to God but to the worshipper so that he or she can make the prayers their own. Silence, used sparingly in the extreme, must not be forgotten. Prayers led by the minister, whether read or extemporised, require the most careful preparation and should be structured in a manner familiar to the congregation, enabling them to structure their own private prayers so that the different parts of prayer – Invocation, Thanksgiving, Confession, Petition, Intercession – are not forgotten. Of course this is well known to every minister but I mention it now to indicate to the man in the pew, as to the man in the street, that the minister's is a very real job, demanding its own appropriate techniques and calling for its own requisite craftsmanship.

In most cases the man in the street is unlikely to be impressed. Whatever his job may be the minister is regarded as flogging, however strenuously and persistently, a dead horse. If the Church itself is written off her full-time servants can hardly expect a better fate; and by the majority of our fellow citizens the Church is written off. To some extent, one must admit, with good reason. If you Christians can't agree among yourselves, we are told, you can hardly be expected to further unity in or between nations. Like so many of my fellow churchmen throughout the world I have always felt the weight of this particular criticism. We are all guilty of disobedience to our Lord Whose will it plainly is that there should be one flock, seen to be one, as there is only one Shepherd. By the terms of its constitution the Church of Scotland is compelled to 'seek and promote union with other Churches in which it finds the Word to be purely preached, the Sacraments administered according to Christ's ordinance and discipline rightly exercised; and it has the right to unite with any such Church without loss of its identity on terms which this Church finds to be consistent with these Articles' (i.e. The Articles Declaratory of the Constitution of the Church of Scotland in Matters Spiritual). The quotation makes it clear however that union with other Churches at any price is not to be contemplated. In 1957 the so called 'Bishops' Report' envisaged a union between Anglican and Presbyterian Churches on the understanding, among others, that the Anglicans would take the eldership into their system while the Presbyterians would receive duly consecrated bishops. Why did I, in company with the General Assembly, emphatically reject the proposals? Certainly not because I doubted the usefulness of the office of bishop. In certain of its aspects that role might prove beneficial to any branch of the Church. Unfortunately however the Church of England took and takes the position that it could not be in full Communion with (i.e. in short, fully recognise as legitimate) any Church which lacks bishops duly consecrated by other consecrated bishops. The doctrine in question is that of Apostolic Succession, the claim that the Church is only truly the Church when its officers find their place in an unbroken succession from the first Apostles. To me, as to so many of my fellow Presbyterians, this is to elevate a matter of ecclesiastical structure to a level wholly inconsistent with its importance and with the insights of Scripture. It is not in this exclusive sense that we understand the doctrine of God the Holy Spirit. To put the question as briefly and practically as possible, were full intercommunion to be practised between the Church of Scotland as presently constituted and the Church of England and were there full recognition of Church of Scotland ministerial orders as there certainly is full recognition of Church of England orders by the Church of Scotland, we might well accept gifts of administration from each other. However to unchurch another Communion because it lacks Episcopacy of the Anglican type is tantamount to denying the Reformation, the Pauline and the Biblical claim that Salvation is by faith in the Lord Jesus Christ and not in any one system of Church administration. Of course, if the Church is to be seen to be one then barriers between us must go: but the different parts of the Church should still be allowed to follow their own 'development' as indeed, after the 1988 Lambeth Conference, Provinces of the Anglican Communion are proceeding to do. Provinces which 'break away' to ordain women as priests and bishops may encourage the hope that other doctrinal 'sacred cows' may yet submit, in the Anglican Communion or the Presbyterian or any other, to the plain demands of the Word as the Word is made flesh in Jesus Christ. If we are told, as we are, that such 'break-aways' over the ordination of women jeopardise eventual union with Roman Catholic and Orthodox Communions the answer must be that unless the truth of the Gospel is safeguarded any such union must do more harm than good.

Whether or not the pace of the Ecumenical movement is to slow down or to quicken the work of Christian Evangelism can and must go on. The outsider has very good reason to be critical of the Churches but sometimes at least this is an excuse behind which to find shelter. In any event it is not the Church in any one of its numerous forms that is to be offered in the first instance to those outside but the Lord of the Church. At the very lowest estimate it is worth putting up with the Church just because so frequently, in spite of itself, Jesus is still to be found there by those who seek Him.

The story told of the late John White does not lose its cutting edge. Addressing a street corner meeting in Glasgow, the magisterial churchman found his address continually heckled. Finally the interrupter asked, 'Why should I go to Church? It's full of hypocrites.' 'Correct,' answered Dr White, 'but there's still room for one more.'

Jesus Christ continues His saving work within the Church, in any or all of its branches, in spite of us all. Those of us who are inside have reason enough to feel shame for the Church's betrayal of its Lord, but no less must we bear witness to His presence with us Sunday by Sunday and day by day: nor would we be telling the truth if we failed to claim abundant evidence for the gifts of the Spirit in the life of any congregation, by whatever denominational title it may be known. Here indeed is the proof that the Church, fragmented as it is, is still the Body of our Saviour, empowered in all its manifest weakness to do His work and continually challenged to become, ever more fully, what in reality it is.

The ecumenical movement, I would submit, must be understood to be a call to every Christian believer to affirm his unity with all who, like himself, are in Christ. If we are in love with the Saviour, rather than with our own institution, we shall not be out of love with any who are His in whatever branch of the Church they may be found. As we rejoice together in the one

Lord and Saviour He will surely show us how we are to march together under His banner and serve His cause in this and every land. Mutual recognition rather than denominational take-overs must be our aim. The fact that the Church has many parts need be no hindrance to the task of evangelism, provided that the barriers which signal 'not in Communion' are taken away and the parts, larger or smaller, rejoice to claim what is obviously true, that they have no monopoly of the Saviour and the work of His Spirit. As we cease to confuse unity with uniformity then unity, and no doubt a measure of uniformity also, may well be granted. Precisely because the one Lord is at work in all the denominations we have so much to receive from one another.

This is true in the realm of worship and it is no less true of Christian citizenship in its widest sense. The tasks of Christian citizenship grow no less demanding and the world, which must be our parish, grows smaller year by year. The World Council of Churches and the British Council provide much needed mechanisms to enable Christians of different national and denominational background to share their understanding of the needs of the world and the answers Christian faith should prompt. The love-hate relationship which both bodies so often inspire is an indication of the difficulty any Christian must experience in seeking the mind of our Lord on the problems which confront us both nationally and internationally. We have an example of this when the General Assembly of the Church of Scotland holds its annual meeting in Edinburgh and provides thereby as much of a Parliament as Scotland may yet possess. In recent years the swing to the Left in the Assembly has been marked although it has never been slow to adopt a radical stance in national and international affairs. It has taken a more than resolute man or woman to rise and commend the Conservative Government. When its Leader Margaret Thatcher addressed the Assembly in 1988 she was heard, as indeed was her right, with the greatest interest, and subsequently warmly applauded. Those however who gladly acknowledge her triumphs in the Falklands War as in the battle with undisciplined Trade Unionism and industrial decline were clearly in the minority. I belong to their number. I thank God that at a moment when our country urgently required leadership of a Churchillian courage and decisiveness such leadership was found. Battles no less crucial remain to be won. Christian men and women are certain to differ as to the nature of the campaign required. It ought to be equally certain that their judgement will be conditioned by the realisation that we live in a fallen world in which none is wholly righteous, no not one. The whiter than white political leader will not be found in any of the camps nor will the voter. The humility and prudence born of the knowledge and its concomitant self knowledge are essential components of the realism so urgently required in national and international affairs alike.

A note of such realism has recently been injected by Bishop Richard Harries. In his *Christianity and War in a Nuclear Age* he examines and in my view effectively rejects the case for unilateral nuclear disarmament. It is simply a fact that possession of a nuclear capability has kept the two major powers from war since World War Two ended. Nuclear weapons have been and remain an effective deterrent. It is shallow thinking in the extreme to blame any particular form of weaponry for failures in international relationships. The build up of weapons is the result, not the cause, of these failures. Improvements in relationships must be sought with all the energy and persistence of which we are capable but complete and lasting success is not around the corner. There is no ground in Christian faith for supposing it ever will be. It behoves us therefore to legislate for this situation and to seek the most effective safeguards, the most powerful deterrents to any would-be aggressor. Great hopes were raised by President Gorbachev and at least in some measure they have been fulfilled. Only time will tell whether enlightened policies will win the day in Russia and so time must be taken by those for whom Soviet Russia has for so long been a threat.

Christian citizenship of a more domestic order must betray a like realism. There is small cause for surprise if those who are not Christian behave in a consistently un-Christian way. For the health of society as well as for their own salvation we who seek to follow Jesus Christ must work and pray for the conversion of our fellow citizens and indeed all our fellow men. At one and the same time we must reckon with the unredeemed and take such measures as will protect effectively what is good in our national life from what is evil. It is to be hoped and prayed that more and more Christian men and women will find their vocations in teaching, at whatever level; in medicine; in the study of law and its administration; in politics; in local government; in our Armed Services, Police forces and prison staffs; in the exercise of devoted parenthood. Such a recruiting drive was never more urgently required if the tide of evil is to be stemmed. It is recorded (John 11:25) that our Lord knew what was in man − the potential for evil as the potential for good. Christian citizenship must take the risk of being called a hard-liner because Christians know, or ought to know, what is in themselves as in their fellow men. In heaven Police forces will not be required. They are needed in a big way here on earth. With our Armed Forces they should be constantly in our prayers. They will not make anyone good but they will limit the power of the bad. In a fallen world can we ever hope to do more than hold the line against attack from the power of sin? We search in vain for any word of our Lord to convince us that we can. When Jesus comes again to be our Judge as He is our Saviour, the world as we know it will be no more. Until He comes, and we know neither the day nor the hour, we are to be aware of the power of evil and vigilant to withstand its attack, whether in our own souls or in the life of the nation. As the Christian Church pleads with the world to take the measure of God's love in Jesus Christ, it is bound no less to affirm the evil which holds the world in its relentless grip – one which Christ and Christ alone can release.

In the aforementioned recruiting list ministers were not included. Perhaps subconsciously I wanted to bring them in at the end of the procession, traditionally seen as the place of seniority. Let me disavow the intention, if it existed. The priesthood of all believers firmly places every Christian on the same level of importance. The proper differentia of the ministry is one of function. You will not be surprised if I claim the function as essential for the life of the Church and the life of the world which the Church is commissioned to serve. Retirement gives me time, too much, to reflect on my inadequacies in my chosen calling but no cause whatsoever to wish for another. Since my schooldays when the assumption first was formed I have never really been in doubt as to what God wanted me to do with my life. When I see my Saviour face to face I shall have small excuse to offer for my stewardship but I shall certainly say Thank you for so graciously and patiently allowing me to do for so long what is, for me, the most fascinating job in the world.